APRÈS

APRÈS

75+ COZY WINTER RECIPES FOR THE PERFECT POST-SKI GATHERING

MAUREEN PETROSKY

Photography by Erin Kunkel

TEN SPEED PRESS

California | New York

For Michael, my favorite

For Mom and Dad, my believers

&

For Chris and Elliot, my reasons

CONTENTS

INTRODUCTION
APRÈS ALL DAY

Après ski is the French term for "after ski," and it refers to the time when everyone gets off the mountain, sheds their gear, and changes into comfy clothes. For some, the ritual involves relaxing by the fire. For others, it means heading out to the local bar to imbibe. Usually, there is music, and always, there is community.

Après ski is a global phenomenon. All over Europe, North America, Japan, even parts of South America and the Middle East, there is ski culture, and with that comes, you guessed it, après ski scenes. And you don't even need to ski to après ski! Although the fanfare around après ski began with world-class skiing, now it's being stoked by breathtaking mountain views, amazing cocktails, great food, live music, luxury hotels, and one-of-a-kind party experiences.

Some of the most famous après spots across the globe are frequented solely for their après scenes. In places like Whistler, British Columbia, you can enjoy an evening full of cozy cocktails, chunky sweaters, and charcuterie boards at the ski lodge, skiing optional. At La Folie Douce in the French Alps, you can step off the slopes, click out of your skis, and belly up to a shot ski, while one of the world's greatest DJs spins for you and a few hundred of your closest friends. Or you can get a little more intimate in Aspen, Colorado, with Champagne coupes, caviar, and a setting more like a serene spa than a nightclub.

Après ski is still an occasion, but now *après* is also a verb. You can après. You can go to an après. Either way, it's a whole vibe. Whether you feel like comfort, luxury, or dancing on tables in your ski boots, in the pages ahead, we've got you covered with great drinks and delicious snacks, inspired by these places around the world for whatever après ski style you seek. Grab your friends and let's après!

Here's a breakdown of what's ahead.

SPRITZES AND CHAMPAGNE SIPS

Après ski has always had a celebratory air to it. Whether you're popping the cork for two or twenty, this chapter has all the bubbles and spritzy sips you could dream of clinking with friends and family.

HOT COCKTAILS

Whether you are coming in from the cold or have been tending the lodge fire while the others hit the slopes, hot cocktails are always in style. Grab your favorite mugs, whip up a batch of hot cocktails, and warm up while taking in the view of the snowy vistas.

SHOT SKIS

Partygoers delight in this fun group activity that involves an old ski with multiple shot glasses attached for people to stand side-by-side and imbibe together. This chapter is complete with a step-by-step DIY tutorial on how to make your very own shot ski. No shot ski? No worries—you can still enjoy these tasty shots. All you need is a cocktail shaker, some friends, and a little bravado.

BLACK DIAMOND DRINKS

Just like the black diamond slopes aren't for the faint of heart, these cocktails are serious. This chapter has a mix of classic cocktails with some twists thrown in to keep things interesting. There are also some stiff spirits and fancy glassware for those seeking a more sophisticated après experience.

ZERO-PROOF APRÈS & TONICS

For well-crafted nonalcoholic drinks, this chapter has you covered. These zero-proof cocktails and tonics all skip the booze but not the flavor or the fun.

SNACKS & APRÈS TREATS

Everyone needs a little something to snack on at happy hour, so this chapter has food inspired by some of the most famous après ski spots across the globe. These recipes are all delicious and work great for midday or late-night après ski gatherings. There's spicy, sweet, and savory. Some are super simple, while others require a little culinary prowess, but nothing is out of reach, and all are definitely worth the effort.

53

1

SPRITZES & CHAMPAGNE SIPS

Après ski gatherings naturally have an indulgent air about them. When in doubt about what to serve, bubbles and spritzy drinks are always a win. Regardless of whether your get-together is a family affair or a romantic candlelit event, it's always an occasion for popping corks. From the slightly sweet Hugo Spritz to the bitter and herbaceous Suze Spritz, to the fizzy Rosemary French 75, there is something on this drink list for every bubblehead to toast to. *Clink!*

HUGO SPRITZ

SERVES 1

Spritzes are more than just a style of drink or a simple ratio of bubbly, bitter, and soda. Spritzes reflect their region, and the Hugo Spritz calls the Northern Italian Dolomite mountain range home. In this area, the elderflower grows wild, and its liqueur is plentiful. This lesser-known spritz serves as a lighter, more citrusy drink than its cousins made with Aperol and Campari. Garnished with mint and lemon, this bubbly drink has become a favorite not only in Italy but also at après ski lodges across all of Colorado.

1 oz / 30ml elderflower liqueur

2 sprigs of mint

3 oz / 90ml Prosecco, chilled

1 oz / 30ml sparkling water, chilled

1 thinly sliced lemon wheel

In a wine glass filled with ice, add the elderflower liqueur.

Remove all the leaves from one of the mint sprigs. Gently roll the leaves between your fingers to release their aromas and oils and drop them into the glass. Stir. Then, add the Prosecco and sparkling water. Garnish with the remaining mint sprig and lemon wheel and enjoy.

ROSSIGNOL
ROSSIGNOL

AMERICANO

SERVES 1

If you like a Negroni but are looking for less buzz, this one is for you. This low ABV (alcohol by volume) cocktail is fun served in a big balloon-like bowl glass, like a Burgundy-style red wine glass or even in a wide-mouthed beer snifter instead of the typical highball glass. Use crushed ice to keep this cocktail really chilled for the ideal drinking experience.

1 oz / 30ml Campari

1 oz / 30ml sweet vermouth

Splash of club soda

1 lemon twist

1 orange twist

1 rosemary sprig

In a wide-mouthed glass filled with crushed ice, add the Campari, sweet vermouth, and club soda.

Run the lemon and orange twists around the rim of the glass, skin side in, and twist to release the oils of each over the drink before adding them and the rosemary sprig to the glass for garnish.

SUZE SPRITZ

SERVES 1

Suze, a French aperitif liqueur, is made with the bitter root of an Alpine flower, and this bittersweet, herbal sip conjures the Alps in a glass. It's citrusy and floral but really has a flavor all its own. You can also reduce the Suze and add an ounce of elderflower for a sweeter sip or an ounce of bergamot liqueur for a more citrusy drink if you like. But to get the full effect of this French gentian liqueur, you just have to go for it!

2 oz / 60ml Suze

1 oz / 30ml club soda

3 oz / 90ml Prosecco

1 lemon twist

1 sprig of rosemary

In a wine glass filled with ice, add the Suze and club soda (and any subs, if desired). Stir. Top with the Prosecco. Garnish with the lemon twist and rosemary sprig.

LILLET SPRITZ

SERVES 1

Lillet, like vermouth, is an aromatic fortified wine. It works well with flavors like citrus, berries, and herbs. Here it shines with chilled tonic and a simple lemon twist. Instead of getting its fizz from sparkling wine, this spritz's bubbles come from the club soda and tonic.

1½ oz / 45ml Lillet Blanc

2 oz / 60ml tonic

2 oz / 60ml club soda

1 lemon twist

In a tall glass over ice, add the Lillet Blanc and tonic. Top with the club soda and garnish with the lemon twist.

APEROL SPRITZ

SERVES 1

The Aperol Spritz may be the most famous aperitif in Europe. It's pretty, simple, and perfect for an après ski treat. Bubbly and bittersweet, this quick, easy spritz is also a low-alcohol cocktail for a lighter end to a ski day.

3 oz / 90ml Prosecco, chilled

2 oz / 60ml Aperol

1 oz / 30ml club soda

3 thinly sliced orange slices

Fill a wine glass with ice. Add the Prosecco, then the Aperol, followed by the club soda. Stir. Garnish with the orange slices.

ROSEMARY FRENCH 75

SERVES 1

//

The French 75 gets its name from the gun used by the French during World War I, and it still packs a punch to this day. Gin, Champagne, lemon juice, and sugar all play nicely together, and this classic cocktail gets a kick with the addition of rosemary. It's the perfect toast to a great day on the slopes.

- **1 oz / 30ml gin**
- **1 tablespoon freshly squeezed lemon juice**
- **1 tablespoon Rosemary Simple Syrup (recipe follows)**
- **3 oz / 90ml brut Champagne or sparkling wine of choice**
- **1 lemon twist**

Add the gin, lemon juice, and simple syrup to a cocktail shaker filled with ice and shake until well-chilled.

Strain into a Champagne flute, then top with the Champagne or sparkling wine of choice. Garnish with the lemon twist.

ROSEMARY SIMPLE SYRUP

MAKES ABOUT 2 CUPS / 480ML

- **1 cup / 200g granulated sugar**
- **1 cup / 240ml water**
- **4 to 6 sprigs of rosemary**

In a small pot over medium-high heat, combine the sugar, water, and rosemary and bring to a simmer, stirring until all the sugar has been dissolved. Remove the pan from the heat and let steep for 20 to 30 minutes.

Remove the rosemary and let cool completely, then transfer to a squeeze bottle or a container with a lid, like a mason jar. Store in the refrigerator until ready to use, or up to 4 weeks.

LIMONCELLO SPRITZ

SERVES 1

Limoncello is the shockingly bright yellow-colored liqueur enjoyed as an after-dinner drink throughout Italy. It's sweet and viscous, super lemony, and lovely on its own or in a cocktail. When used in a spritz, it's tangy, fizzy, and super refreshing—especially after you've struggled to remove all the gear you needed to take on the mountain. Bottoms up.

- **1½ oz / 45ml limoncello**
- **3 oz / 90ml sparkling wine, chilled**
- **2 oz / 60ml club soda, chilled**
- **1 thinly sliced lemon wheel**

In a wine glass filled with ice, add the limoncello, sparkling wine, and club soda. Stir to combine. Garnish with the lemon wheel and serve.

KIR ROYALE

//

This pretty, deep red sparkler is the French aperitif of choice and is one of the first drinks up-and-coming chefs learn to make at the Culinary Institute of America's famed Bocuse Restaurant. One sip of this jammy, rich raspberry/blackberry–flavored liqueur with its pop of tartness, and you will understand the allure.

SERVES 1

½ oz / 15ml crème de cassis

3 oz / 90ml brut Champagne, chilled

In a Champagne flute, add the crème de cassis and top with the Champagne.

NEGRONI SBAGLIATO

SERVES 1

This sip, once an internet sensation, is more than just a dramatic pronunciation—it is a mouthful of deliciousness. (To clear things up, it is pronounced *spahg-lee-AH-toh*.) *Sbagliato* is the Italian word for "wrong," because somewhere along the way, a bartender made the OG three-ingredient classic Negroni cocktail with Prosecco in place of the traditional recipe's gin. If you ask me, the bubbles are a bonus.

1 oz / 30ml Campari

1 oz / 30ml sweet vermouth

1 oz / 30ml Prosecco, chilled

1 fat orange peel

In a rocks glass filled with ice, add the Campari and sweet vermouth. Top with the Prosecco.

Take the skin side of the orange peel and rub it along the rim of the glass, then express the oils into the glass and drop the peel into the cocktail.

CHOOSE-YOUR-OWN LAMBRUSCO SPRITZ

EACH SERVES 1

This red wine spritzer starts with Lambrusco, the Italian red wine that comes with a fizzy finish. It is one of the very few sparkling red wines out there, and it serves up black cherry and red berry flavors and ranges from dry to sweet. It's perfect straight from the bottle or served slightly chilled and can be made into many cocktails, including these three versions here. The first version is made with grapefruit and olives for garnish. The second is made with orange juice and Amarena cherries for garnish. Both are fabulous for après sipping; one is just slightly sweeter. The third—what I call the no-frills version because it's a straightforward 50/50 drink—is also lovely and delicious. Frankly, they are all my favorites, so I couldn't include just one.

TRADITIONAL LAMBRUSCO SPRITZ

1½ oz / 45ml amaro

½ oz / 15ml grapefruit juice

3 oz / 90ml dry Lambrusco

1 oz / 30ml club soda or sparkling water

1 to 3 Castelvetrano olives (optional; see Note)

1 grapefruit wedge

In a wine glass filled with ice, add the amaro, grapefruit juice, Lambrusco, club soda or sparkling water, and olives. Stir and garnish with the grapefruit wedge.

Note

Castelvetrano olives are considered the best olives for this cocktail, as they are subtle, sweet, and not overly bitter or briny. If you can't find these, California Sevillano, Cerignola, or Manzanilla olives will work.

SLIGHTLY SWEETER LAMBRUSCO SPRITZ

- 1½ oz / 45ml amaro
- 1 tablespoon freshly squeezed orange juice
- 3 oz / 90ml dry Lambrusco
- 1 oz / 30ml club soda or sparkling water
- 1 orange slice
- 1 to 3 Amarena cherries

In a wine glass filled with ice, add the amaro and orange juice. Top with the Lambrusco and club soda or sparkling water. Stir and garnish with the orange slice and cherries added directly to the glass.

NO-FRILLS LAMBRUSCO SPRITZ

- 1 part dry Lambrusco
- 1 part Prosecco
- 1 lemon wedge
- 1 thinly sliced lemon wheel

In a glass over ice, add equal parts of Lambrusco and Prosecco. Squeeze in the lemon wedge and garnish with the lemon wheel.

ROSÉ SPRITZ

SERVES 1

Rosé all day can catch up to you, but a Rosé Spritz après is perfection. This simple spritzer lets you clink, dance, and enjoy your après your way.

½ oz / 15ml elderflower liqueur

3 oz / 90ml rosé wine, chilled

1 oz / 30ml club soda, chilled

1 thinly sliced lemon slice

In a flute or coupe glass, add the elderflower liqueur, rosé, and club soda.

Run the lemon slice around the rim of the glass and add it to the rim for garnish.

2

HOT COCKTAILS

After a long day of skiing, nothing beats a hot cocktail in hand while you're snuggled up in the lodge watching the snow fall. Hot drinks—meant to be served warm but not scalding for sipping and not slamming—are perfect for single servings or for larger batches for a group. So if you've got a heavy-bottomed pot or slow cooker, break it out. You'll want to serve these cocktails in mugs or heavy glass vessels, but don't be afraid to grab the to-go coffee cups if you'll be entertaining both indoors and outdoors. These drinks are great served by a fireside, for brunch, at sunset, or under the stars, and are even better when enjoyed with friends.

VIN CHAUD

▲ **SERVES 10**

//

In most scenarios, the idea of hot wine isn't so . . . hot. But call it mulled wine and you have a winner every time. *Vin chaud* is simply the French term for "mulled wine," and it's the traditional drink of choice for après skis across the French Alps. Germans have a version called *Glüwein* and in Scandinavian countries it is *glogg*, but regardless of the name, it's typically made with a mix of red wine, sugar, and spices, though modern versions kick it up a notch with additions of brandy, chocolate, or ginger. The key to the perfect mulled wine is the temperature. Keep it *chaud* ("hot") but not boiling. You want a little steam coming off your mugs, but you don't want to boil away the alcohol. I like to keep a batch in a pot on the stovetop or in a slow cooker on low heat so I can continually add to and take from. Bonus: It fills your space with an amazing aroma and keeps your guests happy all après long.

- **2 bottles (750ml each) good-quality red wine**
- **Zest of 1 orange**
- **Zest of 2 lemons**
- **1 tablespoon peppercorns (see Note)**
- **4 whole cloves**
- **3 whole anise (see Note)**
- **3 cinnamon sticks**
- **½ cup / 170g honey**
- **1 orange, thinly sliced**

In a slow cooker or large heavy-bottomed pot over medium-high heat, combine all of the above ingredients and heat until the mixture is steaming. Do not boil. Ladle into mugs or heatproof glasses and enjoy.

Note

Feel free to amp up the peppercorns or anise if you prefer your sip spicier.

SPIKED HOT NUTELLA
WITH TOASTED MARSHMALLOWS

SERVES 2

//

There is nothing more comforting when coming in from the cold than a steaming cup of hot cocoa—that is, until you've had a cup of hot Nutella. Nutella is the creamy hazelnut chocolate spread used for all sorts of sweets, from filling freshly baked croissants and cookies to a fun addition to PB&J, and it's a star replacement for cocoa powder in this drink. This hot cocktail is delicious with or without alcohol, so it's a crowd-pleaser for all ages. Top with some toasted marshmallows, and your après just got a little more indulgent.

- **1½ cups / 360ml milk (whole milk, lactose-free milk, and nut or seed milks all work here)**
- **⅓ cup / 95g Nutella**
- **1 cinnamon stick**
- **4 oz / 120ml bourbon, Frangelico, cacao rum, or chocolate liqueur (optional)**
- **Toasted large or mini marshmallows or whipped cream**

In a small saucepan over medium-high heat, bring the milk to a simmer. Add the Nutella, stirring until it has melted and has incorporated. Add the cinnamon stick and return to a simmer.

Divide the bourbon or liqueur between two mugs (2 oz per mug), if using.

Remove the cinnamon stick from the milk mixture, then ladle the hot milk into the mugs. Serve with toasted marshmallows.

How to Toast Marshmallows

Using a kitchen torch: If you have a kitchen torch, spread 4 to 6 large marshmallows or ½ cup / 60 grams mini marshmallows on a foil-lined sheet pan and torch each side of the marshmallows until they are golden brown. Do not torch the marshmallows in the mug or glass; even if the glasses are heatproof, this direct flame can crack or shatter them.

Using the oven: Place 4 to 6 large marshmallows or ½ cup mini marshmallows on a foil-lined baking sheet and set under the broiler for 30 to 45 seconds until they are golden brown.

MARRAKECH COFFEE
WITH FRESHLY WHIPPED CHANTILLY

SERVES 2

//

Spiked coffees are a staple around the world: Irish coffee is spiked with Irish whiskey; Italians go for Grappa or sambuca in their Caffè Corretto; and in Spain, the Carajillo combines brandy or rum with strong brewed coffee. Alcoholic beverages are not traditionally common in Muslim countries like Morocco, but a coffee experience I had in Marrakech inspired me to create this boozy version. The famous Bacha Coffee room serves some of the best coffee in the world and is perhaps one of the most gorgeous spots to sip it. People queue up for hours in advance to spend the morning there. Each personalized pot of coffee is served in a shiny copper pot with a bowl of fresh vanilla chantilly on the side. Vanilla beans, stored in individual grinders like mini peppermills for sprinkling on top, make the experience one of a kind. This Marrakech-inspired hot coffee cocktail is perfect for your next après ski sip.

8 to 12 oz / 240 to 360ml hot, freshly brewed coffee

4 oz / 120ml Kahlúa

Freshly whipped Homemade Vanilla Chantilly (see page 44)

To prevent your glasses from cracking, rinse your mugs or glasses with hot water to take the chill off.

Fill each glass about three-quarters high with the coffee and split the Kahlúa evenly between the two glasses. Dollop the whipped chantilly on top (see Note) and enjoy while it's hot!

Note

Lightly whipped cream can break down easily, so pour it slowly over a warm spoon rather than directly onto the coffee's surface. This takes some practice. A foolproof fix is to whip the cream to medium-stiff peaks so you can dollop it gently on top instead.

CONTINUED

HOMEMADE VANILLA CHANTILLY

MAKES 2 CUPS / 480ML

My childhood friend Christy's mother, Mrs. Cino, always topped her hot cocoa with freshly whipped cream. To me, this was the ultimate indulgence, and now, as an adult, I consider hot cocktails topped with freshly whipped cream to be the ultimate treat. Once I finally realized how simple it was to master whipping cream, I never went back to canned (and I promise, once you taste this, you won't either).

For this recipe, you can use a stand mixer and a metal bowl, fitted with the whisk attachment; a handheld electric mixer; or just a whisk and a large clean metal or glass bowl.

- 1 cup / 240ml heavy whipping cream, cold
- 1 tablespoon / 8g confectioners' sugar, sifted, plus more as needed
- ½ vanilla bean, seeds scraped
- Vanilla or almond extract (optional)

In a clean bowl, combine the cream, sugar, and vanilla bean seeds. Taste and adjust for sweetness. While the cream is still liquid, add a flavoring, if using.

Start beating or whisking and continue until you see the cream begin to double in size and start to cling to your beater or whisk. In the beginning, it may seem like nothing is happening, especially if you are whisking by hand. The process happens fairly quickly, so if you are using a machine, don't crank it up and walk away.

Once the mixture has tripled in size and you have a solid, light, fluffy mix that is not liquid or oozing, you're finished.

Note

The key is not to overmix or you'll end up with curdled cream; don't undermix either or you'll have a runny mess. If you have doubts, it's better to stop whipping the cream once you have achieved soft peaks (the peaks will softly fold over when the beater or whisk is removed). You can always hand whisk a couple of times right before serving to bring the cream to stiff peaks—when the cream stands at attention—but you can't salvage overwhipped cream.

HOPSCOTCH

SERVES 2

This recipe was inspired by a sip my friend Belinda raved about having while skiing in Vermont. With a mountain backdrop, some dry, fuzzy socks, and a crackling fire blazing, the warm caramel-apple aroma of this hot cocktail wafting through the lodge will be all you need to cap off a great day of skiing.

- 2 oz / 60ml spice rum
- 2 oz / 60ml butterscotch schnapps
- 8 oz / 240ml hot apple cider
- 2 cinnamon sticks (optional)
- 2 whole star anise (optional)

To each heatproof mug or glass, add half the rum, half the schnapps, and half the hot cider. Serve with a cinnamon stick and star anise, if using.

FRESH GINGER & MAKRUT LIME HOT TODDY

SERVES 2

//

The hot toddy is a must-have in your repertoire for any après ski. It can soothe a sore throat, warm you up, or comfort a tired body after a day on the slopes. Traditionally, toddies are made of whiskey, lemon, and honey, but they're easy to modify to your liking. This version spices things up with a bit of fresh ginger and Makrut lime leaves for layered flavors.

- **1 cup / 240ml water**
- **4 to 6 thin slices fresh ginger, plus some slices for garnish**
- **6 Makrut lime leaves, coarsely chopped plus some whole for garnish**
- **3 oz / 90ml rye whiskey**
- **4 teaspoons honey**
- **Juice from 2 lemon wedges**

In a teapot or small saucepan over high heat, combine the water, ginger, and lime leaves. Heat the water until the teapot whistles or the water starts steaming, then remove the pot from the heat and let steep for 5 minutes.

While the mixture is steeping, divide the whiskey, honey, and lemon juice between two heatproof mugs or glasses.

Strain the ginger-lime–infused hot water, then pour it into each mug. Stir to dissolve the honey, garnish with some ginger slices and whole lime leaves, and enjoy.

Note

The Spoon Trick: When pouring any piping-hot boiling liquid into a glass (even if it claims to be heatproof), place a spoon in it first to prevent the glass from cracking.

SPIKED PEPPERMINT HOT COCOA
WITH HOMEMADE MERINGUE

SERVES 2

//

As soon as you mention après ski, inevitably someone will ask if there will be hot cocoa. My answer is: Of course! I took inspiration from my favorite hot cocoa spot in Yardley, Pennsylvania, called Panna, which tops their cocoa with silky, gooey homemade meringue. This boozy adult version makes for an extra-decadent sip with a kick.

- **2 cups / 475ml milk (whole milk, lactose-free milk, and nut or seed milks all work here)**
- **3 tablespoons Dutch-processed cocoa powder**
- **¼ cup / 50g granulated sugar**
- **Pinch of kosher salt**
- **3 oz / 90ml peppermint schnapps or peppermint vodka**
- **Marshmallow Meringue (recipe follows)**
- **Graham crackers, for serving (optional)**

In a small saucepan over medium heat, combine the milk, cocoa powder, sugar, and salt. Stay close by the stove because milk can quickly boil over. Whisk until smooth, creamy, and steaming but not boiling.

Divide the cocoa and peppermint schnapps or peppermint vodka between two heatproof cups and stir to mix.

Top each with the meringue and serve alongside a plate of graham crackers, if desired.

CONTINUED

SPIKED PEPPERMINT HOT COCOA
WITH HOMEMADE MERINGUE, CONTINUED

MARSHMALLOW MERINGUE

MAKES 1 CUP / 240ML

- **2 egg whites, at room temperature**
- **¼ teaspoon cream of tartar**
- **½ cup / 100g granulated sugar**
- **¼ cup / 80g light corn syrup**
- **¼ cup / 60ml water**
- **1 teaspoon vanilla extract**

In the bowl of an electric mixer fitted with the whisk attachment, or in a large bowl with a hand mixer, combine the egg whites and cream of tartar and beat on high speed until soft peaks form. Set aside.

In a small saucepan over high heat, combine the sugar, corn syrup, and water. Bring to a boil, stirring to dissolve the sugar. Cook for 2 to 3 minutes, then remove the pan from the heat and stir in the vanilla.

Returning to the egg white mixture, turn the mixer to medium-low speed, then very, very slowly add the sugar mixture to the bowl and beat until just incorporated. Increase the speed to medium-high and beat until glossy stiff peaks form, about 4 minutes.

Scoop the meringue into a plastic pastry bag. Cut the tip of the bag so a large layer of meringue will come out when squeezed. Squeeze on top of each cup of the cocoa.

If you have one and you're feeling fancy, you can use a kitchen torch to toast the meringue to a golden brown, or you can simply sprinkle cocoa powder or chopped peppermint candies on top.

CHAMOMILE & RYE
WITH HONEY SYRUP

//

This is an alternate version of a hot toddy, a warm drink made with whiskey and honey. Using chamomile tea adds a layer of complexity, making it extra soothing after a day on the slopes. Rye whiskeys are the perfect addition to a hot toddy, as their flavors range from robust and spicy to smooth with vanilla and caramel flavors. The key to making this sip suit you is how long you steep your tea. The longer you steep the tea bag or loose leaves, the stronger your tea flavor.

SERVES 2

- **6 tablespoons loose chamomile tea, placed in a tea strainer, or 2 tea bags (see Note)**
- **2½ cups / 590ml hot water**
- **3 oz / 90ml rye whiskey**
- **4 teaspoons Honey Syrup (recipe follows)**
- **Juice of 2 lemon wedges**
- **2 lemon wedges**

In two heatproof glasses or mugs, add equal parts of the tea and hot water and steep accordingly. Once steeped, remove the tea strainer or discard the tea bags. Divide the whiskey, Honey Syrup, and lemon juice equally between the glasses and stir to combine. Garnish each with a lemon wedge and serve.

Note

If you prefer more chamomile flavor, steep your tea for five to seven minutes. For a lighter, brighter sip, steep your tea for less time, closer to three to five minutes.

CONTINUED

CHAMOMILE & RYE
WITH HONEY SYRUP, CONTINUED

HONEY SYRUP

This is a simple syrup made with honey in place of granulated sugar. This syrup can be used in any recipe that calls for simple syrup if you prefer the flavor of honey.

MAKES 1 CUP / 240ML

- **½ cup / 170g honey**
- **½ cup / 120ml water**
- **2 teaspoons vanilla extract (optional)**

In a small saucepan over medium-high heat, combine the honey and water and heat until the honey is fully liquid. Stir until evenly mixed. Remove the pan from the heat and let cool completely. If you want a little vanilla kick to your syrup, stir in the vanilla extract once cool. Cover and store in the refrigerator until ready to use, or up to 4 weeks.

If your mixture becomes crystallized or too solid for mixing after being stored, microwave it at 10-second intervals, stirring after each, until the mixture becomes clear and liquid again.

HOT RUM CHAI SOY LATTE

SERVES 2

The warm spices in a chai syrup are intoxicating on their own. Mix them with some silky soy milk and spiced rum, and you've got a perfect hot sip after coming in off the slopes.

- **¼ cup / 60ml chai syrup, homemade (recipe follows) or store-bought**
- **½ cup / 120ml unsweetened soy milk**
- **1½ oz / 45ml spiced rum**
- **Whipped cream, ground cinnamon, or grated fresh nutmeg, for serving (optional)**

In a small saucepan over medium-high heat, warm the chai syrup and soy milk until steaming. (You can froth the milk, if desired.) Remove the pan from the heat and stir in the rum. Pour into your favorite mugs and serve with the whipped cream, if using.

CONTINUED

HOT RUM CHAI SOY LATTE, CONTINUED

HOMEMADE CHAI SYRUP

MAKES ¾ CUP / 160ML

- **1 cup / 240ml water**
- **3 tablespoons brown sugar or maple syrup, plus more as needed**
- **2 cinnamon sticks**
- **6 whole cloves**
- **10 black peppercorns**
- **8 cardamom pods, lightly crushed**
- **1¼-inch- / 6mm-thick piece fresh ginger, thinly sliced**
- **2 black tea bags, or 2 teaspoons loose black tea**
- **½ teaspoon vanilla extract (optional)**

In a small saucepan over high heat, combine the water, brown sugar or maple syrup, cinnamon sticks, cloves, peppercorns, cardamom, and ginger. Bring to a boil, then turn down the heat and simmer for 8 minutes.

Add the tea, remove the pan from the heat, and let steep for 5 minutes. Stir in the vanilla, if using.

Strain into a jar or bottle, let cool on the counter, then cover and store in the refrigerator until ready to use, or up to 1 week.

JÄGERTEE

SERVES 8 TO 10

This traditional après ski punch is often referred to as hunter's tea. Both skiers and hunters alike enjoy this warm drink outdoors after a day of activities. There are as many versions of this sip as there are peaks in the Alps. Most have rum, some spices, and tea. Some have wine, some don't. This recipe makes a large batch of the more traditional warm drink, but it can also be imbibed as a cold shot.

- **2½ qt / 2.4L water**
- **⅔ cup / 55g loose black tea**
- **⅓ cup / 70g packed brown sugar, plus more as needed**
- **5 cinnamon sticks**
- **8 whole cloves**
- **1¼ cups / 300ml dark rum**
- **1¼ cups / 300ml plum or apple schnapps**

In a large pot over high heat, bring the water to a boil, then add the tea. Remove the pan from the heat and let steep for 4 to 6 minutes.

Strain the tea into another large pot to reheat later or into a slow cooker turned to low heat to keep warm throughout the day or evening.

Stir in the sugar and add the cinnamon sticks, cloves, rum, and schnapps. Taste and add more sugar, if desired. Keep warm over low heat and ladle into heatproof mugs when ready to serve.

3

SHOT SKIS

For the uninitiated, shot skis are made up of a ski with shot glasses attached to it. Designed for group imbibing, you and up to three friends line up together along the ski and take the shots at the same time. Skiing is not a prerequisite for enjoying a shot ski—this communal clinking has transcended the mountains and entered bars, bar mitzvahs, wedding receptions, and birthday bashes across the globe. It can often upstage the main event: Its mere sighting can cause a riotous reaction, making it the perfect addition to any après where a full-on party atmosphere is the goal. This chapter is not for the cozy lodge crowd. DJ, crank up the volume. Bartender, start shaking. It's time to shot ski.

Note: All recipes in this chapter will provide amounts for one shot and for four shots (the amount that a cocktail shaker can hold, and the amount that the typical shot ski can accommodate).

HOW TO DIY A SHOT SKI

Shot skis are usually made from retired skis. With piles of old gear hanging about in lodges, what better way to make use of them than to line up shot glasses and drink along with friends after a long day on the slopes? If you have an old ski lying around, try making one of your very own.

WHAT YOU'LL NEED TO MAKE A SHOT SKI

- Old ski, wiped clean
- Measuring tape
- 4 shot glasses
- Drill with 1⅞-inch / 4.76cm drill bit
- 4 (½- to 1-inch / 1.3 to 2.5cm diameter) magnets, or 4-inch / 10cm adhesive magnetic strip
- Epoxy
- Gloves
- 4 (⅞-inch) self-adhesive clear rubber feet, or furniture bumpers

Measure and mark the four spots on your ski where your shot glasses will go: Measure 18 to 20 inches / 45 to 50cm apart, beginning about 3 inches / 7.5cm in from each end of the ski. At each marking, drill about ¼ to ½ inch / 6mm to 1.3cm deep. Do not drill through the ski; just drill deep enough so your shot glass can sit in the hole.

If you are using epoxy: Attach a magnet to the center of each drilled hole, then use the epoxy to glue the opposing magnet to the bottom of each shot glass.

If you are using magnetic strips: Cut a strip to fit the bottom of each shot glass, then cut a matching magnetic strip to fit into the hole for each shot glass.

Add the rubber feet to the bottom of the ski at even intervals.

Once the epoxy has set (if using), place the shot glasses into the ski holes.

Mix up your shots and have fun!

FIRST TRACKS

"First tracks" is a highly sought-after experience in the ski world, where a lucky skier or snowboarder is the first one to lay tracks on pristine snow. This lovely shot is also highly sought after once you've sipped it. RumChata, known for its sweet, creamy vanilla and cinnamon notes, pairs perfectly with cinnamon whiskey to warm you up, despite its snowy appearance.

FOR 1 SHOT

¾ oz / 22ml RumChata

¾ oz / 22ml cinnamon whiskey

FOR YOUR SHOT SKI (4 SHOTS)

3 oz / 90ml RumChata

3 oz / 90ml cinnamon whiskey

In a cocktail shaker filled with ice, add the RumChata and the cinnamon whiskey and shake until chilled. Strain into your shot glass or glasses and enjoy.

MADELEINE

Some of the most famous après ski stories hail from La Folie Douce, a chain of hotels known across the Alps for their spirited après scene. This shot got its reputation from its hotel in Chamonix, France, once a place where people used to come for the skiing but stay for the party. Now they often come just for the après. Here's your chance to have a taste of the hype, wherever you may be enjoying your après.

FOR 1 SHOT

- **½ oz / 15ml amaretto**
- **½ oz / 15ml Cointreau**
- **1 tablespoon pineapple juice**

FOR YOUR SHOT SKI (4 SHOTS)

- **2 oz / 60ml amaretto**
- **2 oz / 60ml Cointreau**
- **¼ cup / 60ml pineapple juice**

In a cocktail shaker filled with ice, add the amaretto, Cointreau, and pineapple juice and shake until chilled. Strain into your shot glass or glasses and enjoy.

WICKED APPLE

Après ski parties are often teeming with shots of schnapps and Jågermeister. But if you want something a little more fun, try this Wicked Apple shot. It starts with cinnamon schnapps and ends with a wicked cinnamon whiskey kick, all wrapped up in warm, cozy apple cider.

FOR 1 SHOT

2 tablespoons warm apple cider

½ oz / 15ml cinnamon schnapps

½ oz / 15ml cinnamon whiskey

Ground nutmeg, for sprinkling

FOR YOUR SHOT SKI (4 SHOTS)

½ cup / 120ml warm apple cider

2 oz / 120ml cinnamon schnapps

2 oz / 120ml cinnamon whiskey

Ground nutmeg, for sprinkling

In a cocktail shaker, add the apple cider, schnapps, and whiskey and stir to combine. Pour into a shot glass or glasses, top with a sprinkle of nutmeg, and enjoy.

SAMOA SHOT

This shot ski mimics the famous Samoa Girl Scout cookie, which is layered with chocolate and caramel and is rimmed with toasted coconut. This dessert shot is the perfect sweet treat after you burn all those calories in the cold.

FOR 1 SHOT

- **1 tablespoon chocolate syrup, for the rim**
- **1 tablespoon toasted, shredded, sweetened coconut, for the rim**
- **¾ oz / 22ml coconut rum**
- **½ oz / 15ml chocolate liqueur**
- **½ oz / 15ml butterscotch schnapps**

FOR YOUR SHOT SKI (4 SHOTS)

- **3 tablespoons chocolate syrup, for the rims**
- **3 tablespoons toasted, shredded, sweetened coconut, for the rims**
- **3 oz / 45ml coconut rum**
- **2 oz / 60ml chocolate liqueur**
- **2 oz / 60ml butterscotch schnapps**

Put the chocolate syrup in a small shallow dish, then add the coconut to a separate small shallow dish. Take your shot glass or glasses and roll the outside of the rim(s) in the chocolate syrup, then in the toasted coconut. Set aside.

In a cocktail shaker filled with ice, add the rum, liqueur, and schnapps and shake until well chilled. Strain into the chocolate coconut-rimmed shot glass or glasses and enjoy.

BABY GUINNESS

A perfectly poured pint of Guinness is a thing of beauty—that gorgeous black and tan layering looks like a work of art. While this sip mimics the look of those pretty pints, it serves up a sweeter pour more akin to an Irish coffee. Either way, it's fun and delicious.

FOR 1 SHOT

1½ oz / 45ml coffee liqueur

½ oz / 15ml Baileys Irish Cream liqueur

FOR YOUR SHOT SKI (4 SHOTS)

6 oz / 180ml coffee liqueur

3 oz / 90ml Baileys Irish Cream liqueur

Pour the coffee liqueur evenly into a shot glass or glasses until about three-quarters full. Use a spoon turned upside down to slowly pour the Baileys over the top of each glass to create a head. Enjoy.

PALOMA SHOT

In many places, the grapefruit-forward Paloma is more revered than the Margarita. Both cocktails are light and refreshing and promise to wake up the senses. This shot version of the standard cocktail has all the bright citrusy grapefruit flavors but skips the spritz, so you don't have it coming out of your nose after you shoot it. Believe me, it's better this way.

FOR 1 SHOT

- Kosher or coarse-ground salt, for the rim
- 1 lime wedge
- ¾ oz / 22ml blanco tequila
- 1 tablespoon freshly squeezed pink grapefruit juice
- 1 teaspoon / 5ml Simple Syrup (optional, recipe follows)

FOR YOUR SHOT SKI (4 SHOTS)

- Kosher or coarse-ground salt, for the rims
- 4 lime wedges
- 3 oz / 90ml blanco tequila
- ¼ cup / 60ml freshly squeezed pink grapefruit juice
- 1 tablespoon Simple Syrup (optional, recipe follows)

Add the salt to a small shallow dish. Run the flesh side of the lime wedge around the rim(s) of the shot glass or glasses, then lightly dip half of each rim into the salt. Set aside.

In a cocktail shaker filled with ice, combine the tequila, grapefruit juice, and Simple Syrup, if using, and shake until well-chilled. Strain into the salt-rimmed glass or glasses. Garnish with the lime and enjoy.

SIMPLE SYRUP

MAKES 1 CUP / 240ML

- 1 cup / 200g granulated sugar
- 1 cup / 240ml water

In a small saucepan over medium-high heat, combine the sugar and water and heat until the sugar is completely dissolved. Remove the pan from the heat and cool before using. Cover and store in the refrigerator for up to 4 weeks.

LEMON DROP

This is the prettiest little après ski shot I ever did see. Her sugar rimmer is reminiscent of fur-topped boots. Combine that with her butter-lemon color and her sassy citrus bite, and this lil shot ski is ready for the after par*tay*!

FOR 1 SHOT

Granulated sugar, for the rim

¾ oz / 22ml vodka

1 tablespoon freshly squeezed lemon juice

1½ teaspoons Simple Syrup (page 67)

1 lemon wedge

FOR YOUR SHOT SKI (4 SHOTS)

Granulated sugar, for the rims

3 oz / 90ml vodka

¼ cup freshly squeezed lemon juice

1 oz Simple Syrup (page 67)

4 lemon wedges

Add the sugar to a small, shallow dish. Run the flesh side of the lemon wedge around the rim(s) of the shot glass or glasses, then lightly dip the rim into the sugar. Set aside.

In a cocktail shaker filled with ice, combine the vodka, lemon juice, and Simple Syrup and shake until well-chilled. Strain into the sugar-rimmed shotglass or glasses. Serve with a lemon wedge on top or on the side. Enjoy.

POLAR BEAR

This minty cool shot reminds me of the chocolate-covered mint-filled peppermint patty candy. There is a different shot, called the Peppermint Patty, that uses peppermint schnapps, but this recipe uses crème de menthe for a snowy sip. Feel free to substitute peppermint schnapps if that's what you have on hand—either will achieve the same minty result.

FOR 1 SHOT

½ oz / 15ml white crème de cacao

½ oz / 15ml white crème de menthe

FOR YOUR SHOT SKI (4 SHOTS)

3 oz / 90 ml white crème de cacao

3 oz / 90 ml white crème de menthe

In a cocktail shaker filled with ice, combine both liqueurs and shake until well-chilled. Strain into your shot glass or glasses and enjoy.

4

BLACK DIAMOND DRINKS

You don't have to ski or have been to a ski resort to know that the black diamond, a symbol used to denote advanced ski runs, signifies we're getting a little more serious now. These drinks are neither shot skis nor simple spritzes. Black diamond drinks are higher in alcohol, more serious in stature, and not for the faint of heart. For this après, think more 007, less hygge. These are drinks that need glassware, garnishes, and game.

SAKE-TINI

SERVES 1

Imagine soaking in a natural hot spring as the steam rises around you at the foot of a snow-covered mountain while sipping sake. This is the quintessential Japanese *onsen*, or "hot spring," après ski experience. If your après isn't in Japan, you can still transport yourself there with a hot bath and a few sips of this sake martini. There are many styles of sake available to choose from, but go for a dry Junmai Ginjo for this sake-tini. This sake is very versatile—dry, with fruity notes of apple and pear—and light-bodied with a clean finish.

2 oz / 60ml sake

1 oz / 30ml vodka or gin

½ oz / 15ml dry vermouth

1 cucumber slice

In a cocktail shaker filled with ice, combine the sake, vodka or gin, and vermouth and shake until well-chilled. Strain into a chilled martini glass and garnish with the cucumber slice.

APRICOT & ORANGE GIN COCKTAIL

SERVES 1

This cocktail is served at one of the most exclusive French chateaux nestled in Les Trois Vallées, directly on the majestic alpine Bellecôte piste. The bittersweet and earthy French liqueur Suze is mixed with orange and apricot marmalade, delivering a glassful of warming winter fruits and spices that you can enjoy even if you weren't able to score a reservation. So grab your favorite sweater, cozy up by the fire, and take a sip of the good life.

1 oz / 30ml gin

1 oz / 30ml sweet vermouth

1 oz / 30ml Suze liqueur

1 teaspoon apricot marmalade

1 teaspoon orange marmalade

1 large orange peel slice, pith removed

In a cocktail shaker filled with ice, combine the gin, vermouth, Suze, and both marmalades and stir until chilled. Strain into a rocks glass filled halfway with ice. Run the orange peel, skin side in, around the rim of the glass, then squeeze to express the oils into the drink and drop the peel into the glass to serve.

SIDECAR

SERVES 1

This recipe is easily adjustable to your liking once you have these three ingredients in place: Cognac, Cointreau, and freshly squeezed lemon juice. The recipe is for the original vintage version but feel free to adjust the sweetness and acid to your taste once you've got this trio in place.

- **Granulated sugar, for the rim**
- **1 lemon wedge**
- **2 oz / 60ml Cognac**
- **1 oz / 30ml Cointreau**
- **2 tablespoons freshly squeezed lemon juice**
- **1 flamed orange peel (see below)**

Add the sugar to a shallow dish. Use the lemon wedge to rub around the rim of an old-fashioned glass, then lightly dip the rim in the sugar.

In a cocktail shaker filled with ice, combine the Cognac, Cointreau, and lemon juice. Shake until well-chilled.

Fill your glass with ice and strain the drink into the glass. Garnish with the orange peel.

HOW TO MAKE A FLAMED ORANGE PEEL

A flamed orange (or lemon) peel is an impressive bar trick that lends a little smoky flavor to a cocktail. To make one, use a sharp paring knife to remove a piece of the peel from your citrus in a circular manner, starting at the middle and continuing around the fruit. You want only the skin and the oils that are in it, so avoid as much of the pith (the white part) as possible, since it can give your drink a very bitter taste.

Using a match or a lighter, hold the flame over the glass. In your other hand, hold the peel, skin side facing down toward the glass. Squeeze the oils into the flame over the glass. The flame will burst out, so be careful not to have it facing anyone. Once it lights, simply drop the peel into the glass.

VESPER

//

There's often debate over whether the martini is made with gin or vodka. In the beginning, this iconic cocktail was made with gin and vermouth. It wasn't until the mid-1960s in the United States that vodka started to make a play. I learned about this spin on the classic using both vodka and gin from the king of cocktails himself, Dale DeGroff. Add the Lillet Blanc in place of the vermouth and you've got yourself a Vesper.

SERVES 1

- **1 oz / 30ml gin**
- **1 oz / 30ml vodka**
- **½ oz / 15ml Lillet Blanc**
- **1 lemon twist**

In a cocktail shaker filled with ice, stir together the gin, vodka, and Lillet Blanc until well-chilled. Serve in a martini or coupe glass and garnish with the lemon twist.

THE BOULEVARDIER

SERVES 1

//

This drink is a spin on the Negroni. Where gin is the star in the well-balanced Negroni, whiskey takes its place in the glass for a Boulevardier. The combination of bitter Campari, sweet vermouth, and a bold whiskey makes for a rich and easy-to-drink quaff with very few ingredients, perfect for drinking around a game board or when shuffling the deck.

2 oz / 60ml whiskey of choice (bourbon, rye, and even Scotch are great choices here)

1 oz / 30ml Campari

1 oz / 30ml sweet vermouth

1 orange wheel or wide orange peel, pith removed

In a cocktail shaker filled with ice, combine the whiskey, Campari, and sweet vermouth and stir until well-chilled. Strain and serve in a coupe glass or strain over 1 large ice cube in a rocks glass. Serve with an orange garnish.

MINTY G&T

SERVES 1

A gin and tonic is a solid, classic cocktail suitable for almost any occasion, including sipping in a Swiss ski village or while lounging by a frozen lake in St. Moritz. Here we've added some muddled fresh mint for a refreshing drink with an echo of a mojito.

2 lime wedges

4 mint leaves

2 oz / 60ml gin

3 oz / 90ml tonic

1 small sprig of mint

Into a tall glass, squeeze the juice of one of the lime wedges and discard the rind. Add the mint leaves and muddle. Fill the glass with ice. Add the gin and tonic and squeeze in the last juice of the lime wedge, stirring to combine. Garnish with the sprig of mint and enjoy.

SMOKE SHOW

SERVES 1

Mezcal and tequila star in this smoky margarita-like drink. The spicy smoked salt rimmer takes this drink to the next level with a little extra heat, so dip with caution.

- Spicy Smoked Salt Rimmer Mixture (recipe follows)
- 1 lime wedge
- 1 oz / 30ml mezcal
- ¾ oz / 22ml blanco tequila
- 1 tablespoon agave syrup
- 2 tablespoons freshly squeezed lime juice
- ½ oz / 15ml Grand Marnier

Add about a tablespoon of the spicy smoked salt to a shallow dish. Use the side of the lime wedge to run along half of a coupe glass, then lightly dip the rim in the smoked salt. Set aside.

In a cocktail shaker filled with ice, add the mezcal, tequila, agave syrup, and lime juice, and Grand Marnier and shake until well-chilled. Strain into the glass and serve with the lime wedge on the edge of the glass.

SPICY SMOKED SALT RIMMER MIXTURE

MAKES 1 CUP / 240ML

- 1 cup / 240g coarse smoked sea salt (see Note)
- 2 teaspoons chipotle powder
- 2 teaspoons smoked paprika

In a small bowl, combine the salt, chipotle powder, and smoked paprika. Transfer to an airtight container and store for up to 2 months in a cool, dry place.

Note

It's important to use coarse-grained salt because regular table salt, being finer, will make this rimmer too salty. Also, the bigger flakes look prettier.

LYCHEE MARTINI

SERVES 1

Often with après ski, the attire is as important as the event. The same can be said for cocktails, and it's no secret that the sleek, sophisticated martini glass elevates any happy hour. This delicately sweet and floral cocktail made from the magic little lychee fruit serves up a sophisticated, swoon-worthy sip.

- **2 oz / 60ml vodka**
- **¼ cup / 60ml lychee syrup (this is the liquid in a can of lychees)**
- **¼ cup / 60ml freshly squeezed lime juice**
- **1 lychee fruit**

In a cocktail shaker filled with ice, combine the vodka, lychee syrup, and lime juice and shake until well-chilled. Strain into a chilled martini glass. Garnish with the lychee fruit added to a bamboo skewer.

ULYSSES
James Joyce
ALMA FINCA
ORANGE LIQUEUR
Product of Mexico
Hart
Sport Billy Kidd

FERNET & COKE

SERVES 1

Fernet-Branca is an Italian liqueur that tastes like black licorice and menthol. The flavors can be polarizing—you either love it or hate it. But pair it with Coke and it becomes a tall fizzy quaff most beloved in Argentina, where the Fernet con Coca is the unofficial cocktail of the country. It's a drink that both warms up your belly and quenches your thirst after a good run on the slopes.

2 oz / 60ml Fernet-Branca

4 oz / 120ml cola

1 orange slice or twist (optional)

In a tall glass filled with ice, add the Fernet-Branca and cola. Stir to combine and garnish with the orange slice or twist, if using.

DEMI-PECHE

//

Typically, a beer cocktail would not make the lineup for a list of black diamond drinks, but this one is French, so by default, it's a little fancier (and it's delicious). Similar to a Shandy or a Radler, this après ski favorite is a fruity mix of beer and peach syrup. To dress it up, add a fresh slice of peach or two before serving.

SERVES 1

- **2 tablespoons Peach Syrup, homemade (recipe follows) or store-bought**
- **12 oz / 355ml wheat beer, cold**
- **1 or 2 slices fresh peaches (optional)**

In a pint glass, add the peach syrup, then the cold beer. Garnish with the fresh peaches, if using, and serve.

PEACH SYRUP

MAKES 1 CUP / 240ML

- **2 peaches, pitted and sliced**
- **5 cardamom pods, seeds scraped (optional)**
- **1 cup / 200g granulated sugar**
- **¼ teaspoon kosher salt**
- **1 cup / 240ml water**

In a small saucepan over medium-high heat, add the peaches, cardamom seeds and cardamom pods and cook until the peaches are lightly golden brown. Use a wooden spoon or spatula to break them up as they cook.

Add the sugar, salt, and water and stir. Bring to a simmer, stirring frequently for 2 to 3 minutes. Remove the pan from the heat and set aside to cool to room temperature.

Strain through a fine-mesh strainer. Once completely cooled, cover and store in the fridge until ready to use, or up to 4 weeks.

ESPRESSO MARTIKI

SERVES 1

//

This sip serves up a caffeine boost with an unexpected tropical vibe. The original Martiki is a drink that hails from Australia, taking the traditional martini recipe and replacing the vodka with rum. In this version, we keep the vodka and bring in the tiki with a splash of pineapple juice. Instead of simple syrup, we are using orgeat syrup, which has a unique almond and orange blossom flavor and is used in many classic tiki cocktails. In cooking, the adage "What grows together goes together" is a way to ensure you're getting the best flavor combinations on your plate. In this case, the coffee and pineapple are what grow together . . . into this delicious drink with a tiki twist.

1½ oz / 45ml vodka

2 tablespoons espresso or cold brew, chilled

2 tablespoons pineapple juice

1 tablespoon orgeat syrup

In a cocktail shaker filled with ice, combine the vodka, espresso, pineapple juice, and orgeat syrup and shake until well chilled. Strain into a chilled martini glass and serve.

AVIATION COCKTAIL

SERVES 1

This cocktail dates back a hundred years. It looks like a precious gem in a glass, and its layered complexity makes it seem like a crown jewel. Those attributes harken to centuries of old-world tradition, reminiscent of snow-capped palaces tucked into the mountainsides that were once visited only by princes, heiresses, and those with sacred status. Want to feel like royalty? Shake up a batch for a fairy-tale ending to a day on the slopes.

2 oz / 60ml gin

1½ tablespoons freshly squeezed lemon juice

¼ oz / 7.5ml crème de violette

½ oz / 15ml maraschino liqueur

1 brandied cherry or Amarena cherry

In a cocktail shaker filled with ice, combine the gin, lemon juice, crème de violette, maraschino liqueur, and shake until well chilled. Strain into a chilled coupe glass and garnish with a cherry.

APRÈS SKI SWIZZLE

SERVES 1

//

Rum drinks often have a summery vibe, but this tiki drink, created by Nathan Hazard of the Coconut Club in Los Angeles and later appearing in Chloe Frechette's *Easy Tiki* book, offers a wintry touch with the addition of green Chartreuse and rum. Add a little almond-y orgeat syrup and bright pineapple juice, and this becomes a delicious addition to any après soiree.

1½ oz / 45ml lightly aged rum (3 years)

2 tablespoons pineapple juice

¾ oz / 22ml green Chartreuse

1 tablespoon freshly squeezed lime juice

1 tablespoon orgeat syrup

1 pineapple wedge or frond

In a tall tiki glass, combine the rum, pineapple juice, Chartreuse, lime juice, and orgeat syrup and top with crushed ice. Swizzle with a swizzle stick or bar spoon until well-chilled. Garnish with the pineapple wedge or frond and enjoy.

5

ZERO-PROOF APRÈS & TONICS

These days, stocking your bar with zero-proof options is so much more fun than offering a selection of seltzers. Zero-proof, no-proof, mocktail, spirit-free, AF (alcohol-free), or N/A (nonalcoholic)—whatever you want to call them, the sips and tonics in this chapter are complex and nuanced.

You will notice some of these recipes incorporate interesting shrubs (a vinegar- and fruit-based mixture that makes an excellent building block for zero-proof drinks), thoughtful garnishes, and even curated glassware.

Whether there are sober guests or ones looking to stay straight for one last run on the slopes, get comfortable whipping up these zero-proof pours so everyone can enjoy something exceptional to sip.

MATCHA FLIP

SERVES 1

//

Matcha goes "après tea" in this bright green elixir with a flip. A traditional flip is a category of drink that includes an egg white to achieve a rich texture with a pretty frothy top. This recipe swaps the egg white for aquafaba, the liquid from a can of chickpeas, which delivers identical results without the worry of using raw eggs. Serve this vegan sip in a coupe glass for a fancy zero-proof clink at any après event.

1 teaspoon matcha powder, sifted to remove clumps

2 tablespoons freshly squeezed lemon juice

2 tablespoons Simple Syrup (page 67)

2 tablespoons aquafaba (see Note)

6 tablespoons club soda

In a small bowl, add the matcha powder, lemon juice, and Simple Syrup and mix well to dissolve the powder. (You can use a matcha whisk, a regular whisk, or a mini frother to mix well.)

In a shaker filled to the halfway point with ice, combine the matcha mixture and the aquafaba and shake until thickened and frothy, 1 to 2 minutes. Add the club soda and strain into a coupe glass. Use a spoon to add the froth from the shaker to the top of the poured cocktail.

Note

One 15.5-oz can of chickpeas contains between ¾ to 1 cup of aquafaba, and 2 tablespoons of aquafaba is equivalent to 1 egg white. To make, drain 1 can of chickpeas through a fine-mesh strainer, reserving the liquid. Whip the liquid for 2 to 3 minutes with a handheld mixer or shake in a cocktail shaker until frothy. Store the remaining aquafaba in an airtight container in the refrigerator for up to 3 days.

MICHELADA

SERVES 2

//

Everyone has a take on this Mexican beer-tail, and it's endlessly customizable. You can swap out the tomato juice with Clamato or a mix of half clam juice and half tomato juice; you can use any hot sauce (try a few until you find your fave!); or if you really need warming up from the slopes, you can crank up the heat even more by adding layers with paprika or a fresh jalapeño slice or two.

- **3 lime wedges**
- **2 tablespoons Tajin or Spicy Smoked Salt Rimmer Mixture (page 83)**
- **¼ cup / 60ml freshly squeezed lime juice**
- **¼ cup / 60ml tomato juice**
- **2 teaspoons hot sauce of your choice (I like Cholula for this recipe)**
- **1 teaspoon Maggi seasoning sauce or Worcestershire sauce**
- **1 (12-oz / 355ml) bottle nonalcoholic lager**
- **6 jalapeño slices**

Run one of the lime wedges, flesh side toward the glass, around the rim of two tall or pint glasses. Lightly dip the glasses into the Tajin or Smoked Salt Rimmer to coat. Fill the glasses with ice, then squeeze the rest of the lime juice from the wedge into the glasses and discard it.

In a cocktail shaker, add the lime juice, tomato juice, hot sauce, and Maggi or Worcestershire sauce and shake until combined, about 10 to 15 seconds

Divide the mixture equally between each glass and top with the lager.

Stir once and garnish with the remaining lime wedges and the jalapeños.

NO-GO SPRITZ

SERVES 1

This is a version of the bubbly elderflower-forward Hugo Spritz (page 16) for the sober set. Instead of the French elderflower liqueur, this spritz swaps in elderflower cordial, which is basically an alcohol-free simple syrup made with an infusion of elderflowers. You can order online or purchase from a specialty store. Skip the champers (but not the mint) and sub in some chilled club soda instead for a refreshing sip.

3 tablespoons elderflower cordial

1 sprig of mint, stem discarded

3 oz / 90ml nonalcoholic sparkling wine, chilled

2 tablespoons club soda, chilled

1 small sprig of mint

1 thinly sliced lemon wheel

In a wine glass filled with ice, add the elderflower cordial.

Gently roll the mint leaves between your fingers to release their aromas and oils as you drop the leaves into the glass.

Stir and then add the nonalcoholic sparkling wine and club soda. Garnish with the mint sprig and lemon slice and enjoy.

ESPRESSO TONIC

SERVES 1

//

Similar to the espresso martini, this drink will give you the energy you need to après all night long. You can use freshly brewed espresso or cold brew concentrate—either gets the job done—but don't skimp on the tonic. Since there are only two ingredients in this cocktail, choose a good-quality tonic that tastes good—nothing too syrupy sweet. If you taste the tonic on its own and you find that its sugar outweighs its quirky quinine, bitter, and citrusy flavors, you can cut it with one part club soda or plain seltzer.

1 shot / 45ml freshly brewed espresso, or 2 oz / 60ml cold brew concentrate

½ cup tonic

In a tall glass filled with ice, add the espresso, then top with the tonic. Stir and serve.

POM TONIC

SERVES 1

This drink is always a crowd-pleaser, and its jewel-toned hue makes it one of my favorite cocktails to serve, especially if I'm hosting an après around the holidays. I like to keep a batch of pomegranate syrup in my refrigerator for this drink alone, but as a bonus, it can take the place of grenadine in any drink that calls for it. It's impressive, delicious, and super simple to make.

- **2 tablespoons Pomegranate Syrup (recipe follows), chilled (see Note)**
- **¼ cup / 60ml tonic, chilled**
- **2 tablespoons club soda, chilled**
- **5 to 10 pomegranate seeds**

In a flute or coupe glass, add the Pomegranate Syrup. Top with the chilled tonic and club soda.

Top with the pomegranate seeds for garnish and enjoy.

Note

If you already have plain simple syrup on hand, you can combine ¾ cup / 175ml of pomegranate juice with ¼ cup / 60ml of simple syrup and shake to combine for a quick fix.

POMEGRANATE SYRUP

MAKES 1 CUP / 240ML

2 cups / 480ml pomegranate juice

¼ cup / 50g granulated sugar

3 or 4 drops of orange flower water (optional)

In a medium saucepan over medium-high heat, add the pomegranate juice and sugar and bring to a simmer. Cook down, uncovered, until reduced by half. This will take 20 to 30 minutes. Be sure not to over-reduce or your syrup will become too thick.

Remove the pan from the heat and add the orange flower water, if using. Allow to cool completely. Skim any foam off the top and discard.

Add the cooled syrup to a squeeze bottle or a container with a lid and store in the refrigerator for up to 4 weeks.

When ready to use: If your syrup is too thick when you take it out of the refrigerator, you can microwave it in 10-second intervals, stirring or shaking after each time, until it is loose and easy to pour or mix.

SHISO SONIC

SERVES 1

This cocktail is a fave at the famous fridge bar, aka Bar Gyu in Niseko, Japan. It's originally made with vodka and/or sake; shiso, a type of basil leaf that has a minty quality; and a mash-up of soda and tonic water referred to as a Sonic. Here is a zero-proof version.

6 shiso leaves, plus 1 shiso leaf, for garnish (see Note)

1 tablespoon freshly squeezed lime juice

2 tablespoons elderflower syrup

¼ cup / 60ml tonic

¼ cup / 60ml club soda

In a tall glass, muddle the shiso leaves, lime juice, and elderflower syrup together.

Add ice to fill the glass halfway, then add the tonic and club soda. Garnish with the shiso leaf and enjoy.

Note

If you can't find fresh shiso leaves, you can substitute with a combination of half basil and half mint or all of one or the other if that's what you have on hand.

MANGO GINGER MULE

SERVES 1

//

Moscow Mules, no matter the flavor, are mules because of those darling copper mugs they are served in. This version showcases a fresh mango and a ginger shrub, but you can easily swap the shrub and club for 6 oz / 180ml of ginger beer if you're in a pinch. If you use ginger beer, just make sure to omit the simple syrup or you'll end up with an overly sweet drink.

- 6 fresh mint leaves
- ¼ cup freshly squeezed lime juice
- 1 tablespoon Simple Syrup (page 67)
- 2 tablespoons Ginger Shrub (recipe follows)
- ½ cup / 120ml club soda
- 2 fresh mango slices
- 1 lime wheel
- 1 sprig of mint

In a mule mug, highball glass, or pint glass, muddle the mint leaves, lime juice, and Simple Syrup together. Add the Ginger Shrub and stir, then add ice and top with the club soda. Garnish with the mango slices, lime wheel, and mint sprig.

GINGER SHRUB

MAKES 1¼ CUPS / 300ML

- ¾ cup / 90g chopped fresh ginger
- ½ cup / 120ml apple cider vinegar
- ½ cup / 100g granulated sugar

In a small glass mixing bowl or 1-quart glass mason jar, combine the ginger, vinegar, and sugar and stir. Cover and let sit for up to 4 days in the fridge before using. The longer the ginger stays in the vinegar-sugar mixture, the more ginger-forward your shrub will be.

Strain and store in the refrigerator for up to 6 months.

ANGOSODA

▲ **SERVES 1**

//

The Angosoda, made with Angostura bitters, was Julia Child's favorite nonalcoholic aperitif (see Note). This drink first appeared in the cookbook *Julia Child & Company*, published in 1978. In addition to Angostura, Julia's preferred, bitters come in many brands and flavors that include lemon, grapefruit, mint, cherry, plum, and chocolate. Experiment and enjoy!

¾ cup / 180ml sparkling water, such as Perrier

4 to 6 dashes of Angostura aromatic bitters

1 lime wedge

Fill a large wine glass halfway with ice cubes. Add the sparkling water and then the bitters. Stir. Garnish with the lime wedge and serve.

Note

Most traditional bitters include a small amount of alcohol, but this drink is still considered nonalcoholic because the bitters are very much diluted. However, if you want to stick to 100 percent zero-proof, source an alcohol-free brand of aromatic bitters.

CITRUSY CUCUMBER TONIC

SERVES 1

This tonic starts with a citrusy shrub that I keep a batch of in the fridge at all times for quick cocktails that always deliver on full flavor. Infused with loads of cucumber, this drink is perfect for quenching your thirst after a hard day of work on the slopes, and the garnish is like a little snack, too.

3 thinly sliced cucumber slices

½ cup / 75g cucumber, diced

¼ cup / 60ml Citrusy Shrub (recipe follows)

¼ cup / 60ml tonic

¼ cup / 60ml club soda

Line a large glass with the three cucumber slices, then fill the glass with ice to keep the slices in place.

In a cocktail shaker, muddle the cucumber and shrub.

Pour the shrub-cucumber mixture through a fine-mesh strainer into the lined, ice-filled glass. Top with the tonic and club soda and enjoy.

CONTINUED

CITRUSY CUCUMBER TONIC, CONTINUED

CITRUSY SHRUB

MAKES ABOUT 2 CUPS / 480ML

- **4 to 6 lemons**
- **6 tablespoons / 75g granulated sugar**
- **¼ cup / 60ml freshly squeezed lime juice**
- **6 tablespoons / 90ml white balsamic or rice wine vinegar**

Use a vegetable peeler to peel the lemons. Do not press hard, as you only want the yellow part of the peel. Set the peeled lemons aside.

Place all the peels into a nonreactive bowl—glass is perfect—then add the sugar. Muddle the sugar and the peels and cover with plastic wrap until the sugar has turned to a syrup. This can take from 1 hour to overnight, depending on the temperature of your workspace.

Juice the lemons; you should end up with about 1 cup / 240ml to 1½ cups / 360ml. Strain the the lemon juice into the sugar-peel syrup.

Add the lime juice and vinegar and stir to combine. Discard the peels and pour into a nonreactive jar, like a mason jar with a fitted lid, and store in the refrigerator for up to 4 weeks.

SPEZI

SERVES 1

This is a super simple, fizzy, zero-proof drink often sold in ready-to-drink cans in Germany and poured up in ski huts across Austria and the Bavarian Alps. With an easy mix of two sodas, you can effortlessly re-create this popular ski slope favorite stateside.

3 ounces / 90ml cola, chilled

3 ounces / 90ml orange soda, chilled

1 lemon wedge or orange slice

In a tall glass filled halfway with ice, combine the cola and orange soda. Garnish with the lemon wedge or orange slice and enjoy.

SKIWASSER

SERVES 1

This drink's name translates to "ski water," and it's a perfectly chilled nonalcoholic choice when getting off the mountain. Use store-bought raspberry syrup or make your own to get that pretty raspberry-red hue.

- **3 tablespoons Raspberry Syrup (recipe follows)**
- **2 tablespoons freshly squeezed lemon juice**
- **¾ cup / 175ml sparkling water, chilled, plus more as needed**
- **1 thinly sliced lemon wheel**

In a tall glass filled halfway with ice, add the Raspberry Syrup and lemon juice. Top with the sparkling water and stir to combine. Garnish with the lemon wheel and serve.

RASPBERRY SYRUP

MAKES 1½ CUPS / 360ML

- **1 cup / 240ml water**
- **½ cup / 100g granulated sugar**
- **½ cup / 60g raspberries**

In a small saucepan over medium heat, combine the water, sugar, and raspberries. Cook for 5 to 7 minutes, until the sugar has completely dissolved and the raspberries have begun to break down. Using a wooden spoon, crush the berries if needed.

Remove the pan from the heat and use a fine-mesh strainer to strain out the seeds and any remaining pulp. Cool, then store in an airtight container in the refrigerator for up to 4 weeks.

6

SNACKS & APRÈS TREATS

Après ski is famous from France to Canada and from Aspen to Austria. The snacks and sweets in this chapter are inspired by the foods found at different après spots around the world and are some of the most comforting dishes you will want to eat when you come in from the cold. Pair them with a drink from one of the earlier chapters to round out a day on the slopes.

CHEESE & CHOCOLATE FONDUE DUO

SERVES 6 TO 8

//

Whipping up a gooey cheese and/or a silky chocolate dip is a fun and social way to warm up frosty faces coming in from the cold. Whether you prefer cheese, chocolate, or both, the options are endless for how you season your dips and what you serve for dunking—don't be afraid to have fun with it! Just remember the only rule for fondue: NO double dipping!

CHEESE FONDUE

- 1 garlic clove, peeled and halved
- 1½ cups / 360ml dry white wine
- 2½ cups / 300g grated Swiss or Emmental cheese
- 2½ cups / 300g grated Gruyère cheese
- 2 tablespoons cornstarch
- 1 tablespoon freshly squeezed lemon juice
- ¼ teaspoon seasoning, such as garlic powder, sweet or smoked paprika, chipotle powder, white pepper, ground nutmeg, ground turmeric, or curry powder (optional)

FOR SERVING

- 1 loaf day-old crusty white bread, like French baguette, cut into 1-inch / 2.5cm cubes
- Sliced apples
- Sliced crudités, such as broccoli, radishes, cauliflower, snap peas, celery, and bell peppers

Rub the cut side of the garlic clove all over the inside of a your fondue pot before heating. Add the wine and let it come to a simmer over the heat source.

While the wine warms, in a large bowl, toss the cheeses with the cornstarch. Add the coated cheese to the pot a handful at a time, stirring after each addition, until all the cheese has melted. Add the lemon juice and stir. At this point, add the seasoning, if using, and stir to combine.

Keep warm, not hot, while serving. A fondue pot with a continual low-level heat source is ideal for keeping your mixture from congealing while enjoying.

Serve with the bread cubes, apples, or crudités.

CONTINUED

CHEESE & CHOCOLATE FONDUE DUO, CONTINUED

In a heavy-bottomed pot over medium-high heat, add the heavy cream and heat to a simmer.

Put the chocolate in a metal bowl or in the bowl of a fondue pot and pour the hot cream over it. Stir until well combined and fully melted, then add any seasoning, if using.

Serve warm with your choice of serving suggestions.

CHOCOLATE FONDUE

- **1 cup / 240ml heavy cream**
- **12 oz / 340g milk or dark chocolate, finely chopped**
- **Pinch of seasoning, such as ground cinnamon, ground nutmeg, orange zest, chili powder, or sea salt (optional)**

FOR SERVING

- **Sliced fruit, such as apples, pears, strawberries, and cherries**
- **Marshmallows**
- **Candied fruit and candied ginger**
- **Pretzels**
- **Biscotti**
- **Graham crackers**
- **Pound cake or day-old crusty white bread, cubed**

JAMBON DE PARIS & BEURRE BAGUETTE

SERVES 8 TO 10

Sometimes it's the simplest things that are the most savored. This sandwich consists of only three ingredients: a great crusty baguette, the best butter you can find (meaning high-fat, low-water-content European butter), and French jambón de Paris or any wet-cured, unsmoked ham that's thinly sliced. That's it. One bite and you'll see why this combo is a French classic: It's simple to make, and when sliced thinly, it can feed a crowd.

- 1 (18- to 22-inch / 45 to 55cm long) French baguette (see Notes)
- 6 tablespoons / 85g unsalted European butter, softened
- 8 to 10 oz / 225 to 300g thinly sliced cooked jambon de Paris (see Notes)
- Sliced cornichons, arugula, or chopped chives (optional)

Cut the baguette in half horizontally without completely cutting through the bread. Butter each side generously. Place the ham on one side, top with the cornichons (if using), then close and slice into 8 to 10 servings.

Notes

If you don't have a French bakery nearby, you can turn any grocery store baguette into a crusty loaf. Brush your store-bought baguette with a little water, then pop it into a 300°F / 175°C oven for 10 minutes to toast it. I know this sounds weird, but it works.

Some delis sell a French-Canadian ham that is close to the Parisian version of French jambon. If you can't find French jambon, a lightly smoked dry ham is preferable to a waterlogged boiled ham for this sandwich.

CAVIAR & CHIPS

MAKES 20 TO 24 CHIPS

At certain jet-setting ski spots like Aspen, Colorado, après ski is a fancy affair, geared toward the caviar and Champagne crowd. This appetizer can be as high-end or as approachable as you prefer, perfect at both a glitzy party and a cozy night at home.

1 oz / 30g caviar

¼ cup / 60ml sour cream

¼ cup / 15g chopped chives

Low-salt or unsalted kettle-cooked potato chips, 20 to 24 chips

Place the opened tin of caviar on top of a small tray filled with ice. Place a small nonmetal serving spoon next to the tray.

Add the sour cream and chives to separate small bowls set alongside the caviar.

To assemble, spoon a dollop of sour cream in the center of a potato chip, then add a small amount of caviar and a sprinkling of chives on top.

POUTINE ARANCINI

MAKES MAKES 22 TO 24 MINI ARANCINI AND 1 CUP / 240ML GRAVY

//

Poutine is a Canadian delicacy composed of gravy-smothered fries topped with squeaky cheese curds. This appetizer replaces the fries, wrapping the cheese curds into little fried balls of rice with gravy on the side for dipping.

Making risotto is lovely if you have time to stand around and stir the pot. We don't, so this dish uses an electric pressure cooker or an Instant Pot for speed and ease. Don't worry, the risotto is foolproof made in one of these (I promise!), and once you figure it out, it will be the only way you make it for this dish or any other ever again.

FOR THE ARANCINI

- 2 tablespoons / 30ml olive oil
- ¼ cup / 40g diced shallots
- 1 cup / 200g Arborio rice
- ¼ cup / 60ml white wine
- 2 cups / 480ml chicken broth
- 1 tablespoon / 14g unsalted butter
- ⅓ cup / 30g grated Parmigiano-Reggiano
- 24 (½- inch / 1.3cm) pieces cheese curds
- ¾ cup / 105g all-purpose flour
- 3 large eggs, beaten
- 1½ cups / 150g bread crumbs, panko or Italian-style
- 4 to 6 cups / 950ml to 1.4L vegetable oil

FOR THE GRAVY

- 1½ tablespoons / 21g unsalted butter
- 1½ tablespoons / 12g all-purpose flour
- ½ cup / 120ml beef stock
- ½ cup / 120ml chicken stock
- 1 teaspoon Worcestershire sauce
- ½ teaspoon garlic powder
- ¼ to ½ teaspoon freshly ground black pepper

CONTINUED

POUTINE ARANCINI, CONTINUED

Make the arancini: In your Instant Pot, select the sauté function. Add the olive oil and shallots and cook for 1 to 2 minutes until translucent. Add the rice and stir to coat with the oil. Cook for about 2 minutes. Add the wine and simmer for about 30 seconds, then stir in the chicken broth.

Turn off the sauté function. Close and lock the lid. Select high pressure and set the timer for 6 minutes. Allow 5 to 10 minutes for the pressure to build.

Release the pressure carefully, using the quick-release method, for about 5 minutes, following the manufacturer's instructions. Then carefully unlock and remove the lid.

Add the butter and stir until the risotto is creamy, about 1 minute. Add the grated cheese and stir until melted and well combined.

Spread the rice mixture onto the bottom of a 9 by 13-inch / 23 by 33cm baking dish. Cool on the counter for 20 minutes and then place the pan in the fridge to cool for another 20 minutes.

Assemble and cook the arancini: Scoop out 1 heaping tablespoon of the cooled risotto, about 1 oz / 30g, and flatten into your palm. Place one of the pieces of cheese curd in the center and wrap the risotto around it to form a ball. Repeat with the remaining risotto and cheese curds. Return the baking dish with the risotto balls to the fridge and chill for 20 minutes or overnight until ready to fry.

Place the flour, eggs, and bread crumbs in three separate, shallow bowls. When ready to cook, roll each ball in the flour, dip it into the beaten eggs, then finally coat it in bread crumbs.

Meanwhile, in a small to medium pot or deep fryer, heat the vegetable oil to 350°F / 175°C using a candy or digital thermometer. (Make sure the oil stays between 340° to 350°F / 170° to 175°C while frying.) Fry the arancini in batches of five or six pieces until golden brown and crisp, 2½ to 3 minutes per batch. Remove the balls from the oil and drain on paper towels.

Make the gravy: In a small saucepan over medium heat, melt the butter, then add the flour and cook for 2 to 3 minutes, whisking continuously to form a light roux. While whisking constantly, add in both stocks. Simmer, uncovered, for about 5 to 6 minutes until thickened. Then stir in the Worcestershire sauce and garlic powder, and season with the pepper.

Serve the arancini warm with the warm gravy on the side for dipping.

GORGONZOLA WAFFLE FRIES

SERVES 4 TO 6

This is the waffle-fry version of loaded potato skins, complete with bacon, Gorgonzola cheese, and scallions. There's no calorie counting here, just pure fun food.

- 1 (22-oz / 623g) bag frozen extra-crispy waffle fries
- 1 cup / 240ml half-and-half
- 1 cup / 100g crumbled Gorgonzola or blue cheese
- 2 teaspoons Worcestershire sauce
- Freshly ground black pepper
- 2 tablespoons sliced chives or scallions
- 4 oz / 115g cooked bacon, chopped

Cook the waffle fries until crispy, according to the package instructions.

Meanwhile, in a small saucepan over medium-high heat, bring the half-and-half to a simmer. Add the Gorgonzola or blue cheese and stir to melt.

Remove the pan from the heat and add the Worcestershire sauce. Season with pepper.

Once the fries are cooked, put them on a platter and pour the cheese sauce over them. Sprinkle with the chives or scallions and bacon on top and serve.

FRENCH ONION SOUP CROSTINI

MAKES 20 PIECES

//

Ooey-gooey French onion soup is fun to eat, but it's not very portable. This version has all the good stuff, but is a much less messy version you can eat with one hand (with a drink in the other).

- **2 tablespoons / 28g unsalted butter**
- **4 cups / 480g sliced yellow or white onions**
- **¼ cup / 60ml red wine**
- **½ cup / 120ml chicken broth**
- **½ teaspoon kosher salt, plus more for sprinkling**
- **Freshly ground black pepper**
- **Cooking spray, for coating the pan**
- **20 (½-inch / 1.3cm) slices French baguette**
- **¼ cup / 56g butter, melted**
- **1 garlic clove, peeled and halved**
- **1 cup / 120g grated Gruyère or Swiss cheese**
- **3 tablespoons finely chopped chives**

Preheat the oven to 425°F / 220°C.

In a large cast-iron skillet or heavy-bottomed pot over high heat, melt the butter. Once foamy, add the onions and toss to coat. Turn down the heat to medium-high and stir occasionally until the onions are a deep golden brown and soft, 20 to 25 minutes.

Add the wine and scrape up any brown (not black) parts from your pan. Cook the wine down for 2 minutes. Add the chicken broth and cook for 3 to 5 more minutes, until the liquid is almost gone.

Remove the onion mixture from the heat and season with the salt and pepper. Set aside.

Spray a sheet pan with the cooking oil. Place the sliced baguette pieces on the pan in one layer. Brush with the melted butter and sprinkle with salt.

Bake the baguettes for 8 to 10 minutes until golden brown and toasted. Remove the pan from the oven and let cool for 5 minutes.

Rub the garlic clove over the top of each crostini. Top each crostini with 1 tablespoon of the onion mixture, then add a generous topping of the Gruyère or Swiss cheese.

Return the pan to the oven and bake for 3 to 4 additional minutes, until the cheese is melted, bubbly, and golden brown. Remove the pan from the oven and transfer the crostini to a plate. Sprinkle with the chives and serve.

RACLETTE BAGUETTE
WITH CURED MEAT & CORNICHONS

//

I always keep a baguette in the freezer, cornichons in the pantry, and cured meats and cheese in the fridge for last-minute entertaining. With little fuss and lots of fanfare, this beautiful baguette dishes up Alpine goodness. Raclette is a Swiss cheese known for being served melty over potatoes with pickled onions and cornichons. Here, I serve it melted on a baguette for an easy pick-up-and-go après treat.

MAKES 12 PIECES

1 French baguette

4 to 6 slices raclette cheese

3 tablespoons Dijon mustard

12 slices cured meat, such as prosciutto

14 cornichons, sliced

Drizzle of honey or hot honey (optional)

Cut the baguette in half horizontally without completely cutting through the bread.

In a raclette pan, on a griddle, or in a nonstick pan, heat the raclette over medium-low heat until it's melty and bubbly with a hint of golden brown.

Meanwhile, spread the Dijon evenly across both sides of the bread. Distribute the prosciutto and the cornichons across one side of the open baguette and drizzle with the honey or hot honey, if using.

Slide the melted raclette off the pan on top of the other ingredients. Close the baguette and slice it into portions.

SPICED YOGURT CHICKEN TENDIES

MAKES 20 TO 22 PIECES

//

Everybody needs a little protein after a day on the slopes, and these chicken tenders are loaded with substance and flavor. If you marinate the tenders ahead of time, you can pop them into the oven when you walk in the door. By the time you've kicked off all your gear, you'll have a nice warm, crispy snack ready for you.

- ½ cup / 120g fat-free plain Greek yogurt
- 2 tablespoons freshly squeezed lemon juice
- 1 tablespoon red wine vinegar
- 1 tablespoon olive oil
- 3 garlic cloves, minced
- 1 teaspoon dried oregano
- 1 teaspoon kosher salt
- ½ teaspoon freshly ground black pepper
- 1½ lbs / 680g chicken tenders, sliced in half lengthwise (about 20 to 22 pieces)
- Cooking spray or olive oil, for coating the pan

FOR THE COATING

- 1⅓ cups / 80g panko bread crumbs
- 1 teaspoon paprika
- 1 teaspoon garlic powder
- ½ teaspoon za'atar

In a large bowl, combine the yogurt, lemon juice, vinegar, olive oil, garlic, oregano, salt, and pepper. Add the chicken tenders and coat well with the marinade. Cover and refrigerate for at least 30 minutes or up to 4 hours.

Preheat the oven to 425°F / 220°C. Line a sheet pan with parchment paper and lightly spray with the cooking oil.

Make the coating: In a shallow bowl, combine the panko with the paprika, garlic powder, and za'atar.

Coat and bake the chicken: Remove a chicken piece from the marinade and roll it in the coating until covered. Continue until all the pieces have been coated. Place the coated pieces onto the prepared pan in a single layer and spray with more cooking oil.

Bake on the top rack of the oven for 10 minutes. Flip each piece, spray again with the cooking oil, then bake for another 6 minutes. Switch the oven to the broiler setting, then put the pan under the broiler for about 2 minutes, or until the pieces are brown (keep a close eye, as some broilers need only 1 minute for final browning). Remove the chicken from the pan and place on a serving platter. Serve warm.

HOW TO CREATE AMAZING GRAZING BOARDS

Grazing boards are exactly what the name implies: large platters of food items that guests can graze upon throughout the night. With a little planning and forethought, they are easy to assemble, make a big impact, and can be a host's best friend when serving a crowd.

The key to beautifully balanced grazing boards is a variety of ingredient options and colors. You also want items that can hang around at room temperature for a couple of hours and are easily replenished. Keep your pantry and fridge stocked with a few items from each category here, and all you need to do on the day of is open packages, place the items on cutting boards, platters, cake dishes, plates, or bowls, and voilà! Your après is about to get a whole lot more impressive.

THE HARD AND SOFT MEATS

Cured hard salamis (pepperoni, soppressata, chorizo, saucisson sec)
Paper-thin sliced prosciutto
Jamòn serrano
Jamòn iberico

THE SAVORY & TANGY

Mustards (Dijon, stone ground, horseradish)
Pickles
Pickled veggies
Raw fresh veggies
Olives
Tapenade
Roasted peppers
Spiced nuts
Dips (hummus, whipped feta, white bean, or ranch)
Fennel slaw
Olive and flavored oils, for dipping

THE SOFT & SPREADABLE

Soft sausages (duck, pork, chicken, rabbit, lamb)
Paté or terrine
Lard
Flavored butters, such as black truffle

THE SWEET

Jams (fig, apricot, honey)

Chutney

Candied nuts

Dried fruit

Fresh fruit (grapes, cherries, pears, apples, melons, oranges)

Chocolate (dark or milk)

Marshmallows

Caramels

Truffles

Cookies

THE CHEESES

Fresh cheeses (Burrata, mozzarella)

Soft-ripened cheeses (Havarti Friulano)

Firm cheeses, such as aged provolone

Hard cheeses (Grana Padano, Parmigiano-Reggiano)

Veined cheeses (blue cheese, Stilton, and Gorgonzola)

THE TRANSPORT

Crackers

French baguette slices

Ciabatta

Breadsticks

Toast

Pretzels

TIPS FOR BEAUTIFUL GRAZING BOARDS

1. For maximum visual impact, make a pile, grouping, or line of one item, then do the same with the next item, making sure they're fairly close together (even touching).
2. Place jams, olives, and nuts in small bowls.
3. Use glasses for breadsticks.
4. Keep grapes in whole clusters.
5. Keep cheeses in whole wedges or wheels; cut a couple pieces to get guests started.
6. Fill in any empty areas with fresh herbs.
7. You may not need utensils but don't forget to put out napkins and cheese knives, serving forks for meats, and small spoons for any dips, sauces, or jams.

FLEUR DE SEL & EVOO FOCCACIA
WITH MORTADELLA, PISTACHIO PESTO & SHAVED PARM

MAKES 16 SANDWICHES, OR 32 FINGER SANDWICHES

//

Focaccia is the easiest bread to make from scratch, but feel free to pick up a loaf if your mountain town has a killer bakery. This freshly baked focaccia can be enjoyed on its own, with a drizzle of high-quality extra-virgin olive oil and some fleur de sel, or made into an amazing sandwich with mortadella, pistachio pesto, and some shaved Parmesan.

FOR THE FOCACCIA

- 4 cups / 560g bread flour
- 2 teaspoons kosher salt
- 1 (¼ oz) packet instant active dry yeast
- 2 cups / 480ml warm water (not hot!)
- 4 tablespoons extra-virgin olive oil (EVOO)
- Fleur de sel, for sprinkling

FOR THE PESTO

- ¾ cup / 180ml packed basil leaves
- ½ cup / 120ml shelled pistachios
- 6 tablespoons / 90ml extra-virgin olive oil
- Freshly ground black pepper

FOR THE SANDWICH

- 14 oz / 400g thinly sliced mortadella
- 3 oz Parmesan shavings

Make the focaccia: In a large bowl, combine the flour, salt, yeast, and water. (Make sure your water isn't too hot, or it will kill the yeast and your dough won't rise.) Drizzle 1 tablespoon of the olive oil over the top. Cover the bowl with a clean kitchen towel and leave out on the counter for 1½ hours or until it has doubled in size.

Spread 2 tablespoons of the olive oil on a rimmed sheet pan or jelly roll pan.

Turn the dough out onto the pan and form into a smooth ball. Toss the ball in the oil, then let it sit on the counter for 2 hours, or until it has spread out and fills the pan.

Preheat the oven to 425°F / 220°C.

Top the dough with the remaining tablespoon of olive oil and use your fingers to dimple the dough while pressing it into the pan evenly. Sprinkle the top with the fleur de sel.

Bake the focaccia for 20 to 25 minutes, until golden brown. Cool in the pan for 15 minutes, then move it to a wire rack until completely cool.

When cool, slice the entire slab open, creating a top and bottom. If you're struggling to cut the bread evenly, use a bread knife to score halfway down the sides of the bread. Continue scoring all along the sides of the bread to create a guide, then cut all the way through, creating your top and bottom.

Make the pesto and assemble the sandwich: In a small food processor, pulse the basil, pistachios, and olive oil until smooth. Season with pepper. Spread the pistachio pesto across one whole open side of the focaccia. Distribute the sliced mortadella across the other side, top with the Parmesan, and place the lid on top. Slice into individual pieces.

POLENTA BITES
WITH SHORT RIB RAGU

MAKES 16 TRIANGLE PIECES

Many mountainside establishments offer the satisfying, rich, and hearty fare you crave after a day on the slopes, and this short rib ragu is just that! The recipe makes enough ragu not only to serve for this appetizer but also enough extra to use for a pasta dish later on or to keep in the freezer for last-minute entertaining. You can make both the ragu and the polenta ahead of time and reheat them right before serving.

RAGU

- 2 lbs / 900g bone-in short ribs, patted dry
- Kosher salt and freshly ground black pepper
- 2 tablespoons extra-virgin olive oil
- 2 cups / 240g chopped onions
- 1 cup / 140g chopped carrots (about 2 carrots)
- 1 cup / 140g chopped celery (about 3 stalks)
- 1 (6-oz / 170g) can tomato paste
- 1 cup / 240ml red wine
- 2 cups / 480ml beef broth
- Several sprigs each of rosemary and thyme

Preheat the oven to 350°F / 175°C.

Generously cover the short ribs with salt and pepper.

In a Dutch oven or heavy-bottomed pot with a fitted lid over medium-high heat, add the olive oil. When the oil starts to shimmer, working in batches, add the short ribs and sear to a golden brown, removing to a plate as they are browned. When finished, remove and discard excess fat until 2 tablespoons remain in the pot.

Add the onions, carrots, and celery to the same pot and cook, stirring until the onions are translucent, about 8 minutes. Add the tomato paste and cook until lightly browned, about 3 minutes more. Add the wine to deglaze the pan, using your spoon to scrape the fond (all the good caramelized parts) off the bottom.

Add the broth, short ribs, and both herbs, and cover. Place the pan in the oven and cook for 90 minutes, checking every now and then to be sure there is still plenty of liquid to cover the meat. The meat is done when it falls off the bone. If needed, you can add more broth or water and cover again and cook for another hour.

When the short ribs are fully cooked, remove the bones, shred the meat, and return it to the pot and mix well. Reserve until ready to serve. This recipe will make more than you will need for the polenta bites.

POLENTA BITES

Cooking spray, for coating the pan

2 cups / 480ml water

1 teaspoon kosher salt

½ cup / 70g instant polenta

⅓ cup / 10g finely grated Parmesan cheese

Freshly ground black pepper

¼ cup / 60ml olive oil

Line an 8 by 8-inch / 20 by 20cm baking dish with parchment paper and spray with the cooking oil.

In a small saucepan over medium heat, combine the water and salt and bring to a boil. Add the polenta and whisk to combine. Turn down the heat to low and cook while whisking continuously for 2 to 3 minutes until the polenta starts to come away from the sides of the pan.

Remove the pan from the heat, add the Parmesan, and season with pepper to taste.

Using a rubber spatula, transfer the polenta to the prepared baking dish. Cool on the counter for 20 minutes, then transfer the dish to the refrigerator to cool completely, about another hour.

When ready to serve, preheat the oven to 375°F / 190°C. Remove the pan from the refrigerator, lift the edges of the parchment to remove the polenta in one piece from the pan, and cut it into sixteen small triangles.

Generously and evenly oil a sheet pan with the olive oil. Place the polenta triangles on the pan. Place the pan on the bottom rack of the oven and heat the triangles for about 30 minutes, or until crispy and golden brown on one side. Then flip them over and cook for 10 more minutes. Remove the triangles from the pan and drain on a paper towel.

Serve with a dollop of warm short rib ragu on top.

SPINACH & SUN-DRIED TOMATO BOUREKAS

MAKES 16 LARGE OR 48 BITE-SIZE PIECES

//

I love a vegetarian appetizer that satisfies both veggie- and meat-lovers. I fell in love with bourekas in Morocco, where they pack flaky pastry dough with all sorts of savory and spiced fillings. Here, olives and sun-dried tomatoes impart a ton of umami, chili flakes bring a bit of heat, and the sesame seeds give a great crunch. This is a simple sheet pan appetizer that looks great and tastes even better. It's a very forgiving and versatile vehicle for a lot of filling options. Keep a box of puff pastry in the freezer and you'll be ready to throw together a snack for any last-minute après guests.

2 cups / 240ml shredded whole milk mozzarella cheese

15 oz (about 1¾ cups) / 430g whole milk ricotta cheese

1 cup / 150g crumbled feta cheese

2 cups / 40g loosely packed fresh baby spinach, coarsely chopped

½ cup / 60g sun-dried tomatoes, drained and finely chopped

½ cup / 85g Kalamata olives, pitted and chopped

½ teaspoon chili flakes

3 large eggs

2 sheets puff pastry, thawed

1 teaspoon water

2 to 2½ tablespoons sesame seeds, for topping

Preheat the oven to 375°F / 190°C.

In a large bowl, combine the mozzarella, ricotta, feta, spinach, sun-dried tomatoes, olives, chili flakes, and 2 of the eggs until evenly combined. Set aside.

Cut two pieces of parchment paper slightly smaller than a sheet pan.

Lay one sheet of puff pastry on each of the pieces of parchment. (One sheet will be for the bottom layer and the other for the top.)

Roll out each piece of puff pastry to a size just barely smaller than the piece of parchment paper. Move one of the rolled-out puff pastries and its piece of parchment onto a sheet pan.

Spread the filling over the puff pastry on the sheet pan. Invert the other piece of rolled-out puff pastry on top, then remove the parchment from that piece.

Using a sharp knife, cut diagonal lines one way across the dough, creating a 2-inch / 5cm diamond pattern, then rotate and cut in the other direction. Be sure that the knife goes all the way through the top layer of puff pastry.

Beat the remaining egg with the water and, using a pastry brush, cover the entire surface with the egg wash.

Sprinkle the surface generously with the sesame seeds.

Bake on the middle rack of the oven for about 50 minutes, or until the puff pastry is puffed up to double its size and is golden brown. If after 30 minutes it is getting too brown, cover it with a tented piece of aluminum foil and continue baking.

Remove the pan from the oven and place on a wire rack to cool slightly. Then cut along the diagonal lines to loosen each piece for serving. Enjoy.

TOMATO SOUP
WITH BUTTERED RITZ CRACKERS

SERVES 8 TO 10

Ever since I was a kid, the best thing for me after coming in from the cold was hot soup, and still nothing beats it. This soup is rich and creamy and topped with buttery Ritz crackers, just like my mom used to serve it. Make a pot before you head out to the slopes for easy reheating or keep warm in a slow cooker so it's ready when everyone comes in the door. Kids and adults in my house love it so much that they barely kick off their ski boots before grabbing a mugful.

- 1 cup (2 sticks) / 220g unsalted butter, softened
- 3 tablespoons olive oil
- 2 cups / 240g chopped onions
- ½ cup / 70g diced carrot (about 1 carrot)
- ½ cup / 55g celery, diced (about ½ stalk)
- 4 (28-oz) cans diced tomatoes
- 1¼ cups / 300ml chicken broth
- 1 to 2 tablespoons granulated sugar
- ¾ cup / 180ml half-and-half
- Kosher salt and freshly ground black pepper
- 24 to 30 Ritz crackers

In a large pot over medium-low heat, melt ½ cup (1 stick) of the butter, then add the olive oil, onions, carrot, and celery. Cook until soft, 15 to 20 minutes. Do not brown.

Stir in the tomatoes, broth, and 1 tablespoon of the sugar and decrease the heat to low. Simmer for 20 minutes, stirring occasionally, being sure to scrape the bottom of the pot each time to avoid burning.

Remove the pan from the heat. Puree the mixture until smooth, either in a blender or right in the pot using an immersion blender. For a smoother soup, strain the mixture, or keep as is for a thicker version.

Stir in the half-and-half. Season to taste with salt and pepper. Taste and add the remaining tablespoon of sugar, if needed.

Butter one side of each of the Ritz crackers with the remaining softened butter, then serve alongside a hearty mug or bowl of the soup.

HOMEMADE EVERYTHING BAGEL SOFT PRETZELS & GRAINY MUSTARD

MAKES 16 PRETZELS

//

Pretzels, wursts, sauerbratens, and beer are staples at ski huts and umbrella bars (casual outdoor-covered bars) across Austria, Germany, and the Bavarian Alps. Pair these warm, chewy pretzels with a great après playlist to create your own ski hut at home.

- **1 (¼ oz) packet instant active dry yeast**
- **1 teaspoon granulated sugar**
- **3 cups / 720ml warm water (not hot!)**
- **2½ cups / 330g bread flour, plus more for dusting**
- **1 teaspoon kosher salt**
- **Cooking spray, for coating the bowl**
- **¼ cup / 56g baking soda**
- **¼ cup / 55g unsalted butter, melted**
- **Everything bagel spice mix, for sprinkling**
- **Grainy or spicy mustard, for serving**

Preheat the oven to 475°F / 245°C. Line two sheet pans with parchment paper.

In the large bowl of a stand mixer, fitted with the dough hook attachment, add the yeast, sugar, and 2 cups / 480ml of the warm water. (Make sure your water isn't too hot, or it will kill the yeast and your dough won't rise.)

Mix to combine, then let sit for 5 minutes until the yeast has bloomed.

Once the yeast has bloomed, turn the mixer to low speed and slowly add the flour, 1 cup at a time. Add the salt and mix until combined.

Knead in the mixer for 4 to 5 minutes, until a smooth ball forms.

Spray a separate large bowl with the cooking oil. Add the dough to the bowl and cover with a clean, dry kitchen towel. Set the bowl aside and let the dough rise until it has doubled in size. This will take about an hour in a warm kitchen.

CONTINUED

Pommery

HOMEMADE EVERYTHING BAGEL SOFT PRETZELS & GRAINY MUSTARD, CONTINUED

Meanwhile, combine the remaining 1 cup / 240ml warm water and the baking soda in a 9 by 13-inch / 23 by 33cm glass baking dish and stir to dissolve the baking soda. Set aside.

Once the dough has risen, turn the dough out onto a clean work surface. Cut the dough in half and then each half in half again, until you get sixteen equal pieces. Roll each piece into a long strip, about 18 inches / 45cm long. If the dough keeps snapping back or is fighting you, let it rest for another 5 minutes.

Once you have your long strips, you can twist or shape the dough however you'd like from here. For a traditional pretzel shape, take each strip and form a U-shape in front of you, and then twist the ends together twice, and bring the twisted part back toward you.

Place each pretzel into the baking soda bath, being sure to coat each side. Shake off the excess water and place onto the prepared sheet pans.

Bake for 8 or 9 minutes, until golden brown. You may have to move the bottom pan up to the top shelf of your oven for the last minute to brown.

Once you have removed each pan from the oven, brush the pretzels with some of the butter, generously sprinkle with everything bagel topping, then brush again with the remaining butter. Serve with mustard.

MINI CROQUE MONSIEURS

MAKES 16 PIECES

//

The key to this sandwich is the sauce. Béchamel, to be specific. Béchamel is one of the mother sauces of French cuisine, and once you master it, you can create dozens of variations. This classic grilled French sandwich is smothered in it, giving the American ham and cheese a major glow-up. The traditional ham used is jambon de Paris, but any ham works for this recipe. To up the ante, add a fried egg to make it a croque madame instead.

BÉCHAMEL SAUCE

- 2 tablespoons / 28g unsalted butter
- 2 tablespoons / 16g all-purpose flour
- 1½ cups / 360ml whole milk
- Kosher salt and freshly ground black pepper
- 4 oz / 115g grated Gruyère, Emmental, or Swiss cheese, or a mix of them
- Pinch of grated nutmeg (optional)

SANDWICHES

- 8 slices good-quality country white bread or brioche
- Dijon mustard, for spreading
- 8 slices ham
- 4 oz / 115g grated Gruyère, Emmental, or Swiss cheese, or a mix of them

Make the béchamel: In a medium saucepan over medium-low heat, melt the butter, then add the flour and whisk for 1 minute. While continuously whisking, add the milk in a steady stream until it is fully incorporated. (It will seize up but then loosen again.) Cook until the mixture coats the back of a spoon, about 5 minutes.

Season with salt and pepper, then add the cheese and nutmeg (if using) and stir to combine. Set aside.

Assemble the sandwiches: Preheat the broiler.

Place the bread on a sheet pan, then slide the pan under the broiler for 30 seconds to a minute on each side to toast your bread. Watch carefully! Some broilers will toast faster and you may only need 20 seconds per side. Once toasted, spread the Dijon on one side of each slice of bread.

Place 2 pieces of ham on top of 4 of the slices of bread and top each with 1 scant tablespoon of the sauce to cover the ham. Place a piece of bread on top of each to make four sandwiches, then slide them back onto the sheet pan.

Cut the sandwiches into four triangles or four squares for a total of sixteen pieces. Spread the remaining sauce over each piece and sprinkle with the cheese. Place the pan back under the broiler for 1 to 2 minutes, until the tops are golden brown and bubbly.

PASTEIS DE NATA

MAKES 12 TARTS

The Portuguese Pastel de Nata, or its plural Pasteis de Nata, is a darling eggy custard, perfect for eating warm or at room temperature. Nestled into a flaky crust, it's just sweet enough to satisfy any craving. This recipe takes a shortcut and uses store-bought puff pastry dough while still achieving a decadent dessert.

- Butter or cooking spray, for greasing the muffin tin
- ½ cup / 100g granulated sugar
- ¼ cup plus 1 tablespoon / 75ml water
- 1 cinnamon stick
- 1 lemon, zested into fat strips
- ½ vanilla bean, seeds scraped
- 1½ cups / 360ml whole milk
- ⅓ cup / 45g all-purpose flour, plus more for dusting
- ¼ teaspoon kosher salt
- 6 large egg yolks
- 2 sheets puff pastry, thawed

Preheat the oven to 500°F / 260°C. Lightly grease a 12-cup muffin tin with the butter or cooking spray.

In a small saucepan over high heat, combine the sugar, water, cinnamon stick, lemon zest, and vanilla bean seeds and pod, and bring to a boil.

In a separate small saucepan over medium heat, whisk the milk, flour, and salt together. Cook, whisking until the mixture thickens, about 5 minutes. Remove the pan from the heat and let cool for at least 10 minutes.

After the mixture has cooled for 10 minutes, in a separate bowl, temper the egg yolks by whisking a spoonful of the milk mixture at a time to the yolks to bring their temperature up slowly. Then, once the egg mixture is warm, add it to the pot with the milk. Then, add the syrup mixture and whisk to combine. Strain the entire mixture through a fine-mesh strainer, then cool completely.

For the dough, stack both sheets of puff pastry on top of each other and roll into a tight log. Cut the log into twelve ½-inch / 1.3cm slices.

Place a slice into each well of the prepared muffin tin. Get a small bowl of water to keep your fingers wet and then, starting from the middle, press each dough slice into the bottom and up the sides of each muffin well to create a small bowl. Be sure to make the dough thin on the bottom so you won't end up with raw dough.

Once the custard has completely cooled, use a spring-loaded ice cream scoop to fill the pastry cups with the custard. Bake for 12 to 14 minutes, until the pastry looks brown and puffy and the custard is just set. Cover loosely with foil to prevent the tops from burning and continue baking for another 15 minutes, until the custard is completely set, the pastry is baked through, and your Pasteis de Nata easily come out of the pan. Cool and enjoy.

MINI MOUNTAINS TART (AKA TOBLERONE TART)

SERVES 8 TO 10

//

There isn't a more après ski treat than this Swiss Alps–inspired dessert, made with a Swiss candy shaped like a tiny mountain range, packed full of honey, nougat, and chocolate goodness. I love to make this tart ahead and put it in the fridge. Pull it out after a long day, and voilà, everyone will be swooning over this decadent sweet.

FOR THE CRUST

- 12 graham cracker sheets (see Note)
- ½ cup (1 stick) / 110g unsalted butter, melted

FOR THE FILLING

- 4 full-size Toblerone chocolate bars
- 1⅓ cups / 315ml heavy cream
- ¼ cup / 55g unsalted butter

FOR THE TOPPING

- ⅔ cup / 160ml heavy cream
- 1 tablespoon / 8g confectioners' sugar

Make the crust: In a food processor, add the graham crackers and butter and pulse to crumbs.

Press into a 9-inch / 23cm springform or tart pan and chill for 10 minutes in the fridge.

Make the filling: Separate the triangles of the Toblerone bar, reserving 8 triangles for decorating the top of the tart. Chop the remaining pieces.

In a heavy-bottomed pot over medium-high heat, combine the heavy cream and butter and heat until just simmering. Pour in the chopped Toblerone pieces, remove the pan from the heat, and let sit for 2 minutes. Using a rubber spatula, stir the mixture until completely smooth.

Remove the crust from the fridge and pour the filling into the set crust. Return the filled crust to the fridge to chill until completely firm, 3 hours or overnight.

Prepare the topping: When you're ready to serve the tart, in a small bowl, combine the heavy cream and sugar and whip to medium peaks. Keep cold until ready to decorate the tart.

When the tart is completely set, decorate it with the whipped cream and the reserved Toblerone pieces and serve.

Note

If you're pressed for time, a store-bought graham cracker crust will work, too.

WARM DUBAI CHOCOLATE CHUNK COOKIES

MAKES 20 LARGE COOKIES

Dubai Chocolate is traditionally milk chocolate filled with pistachio cream and *kataifi*, or "shredded phyllo dough." These cookies use Dubai chocolate as inspiration, amping up the flavors with dark chocolate chunks and sea salt. Think of it as a mash-up of chocolate chip cookies and Dubai chocolate bars. Serve these cookies warm to guests coming in off the slopes, and your ski lodge will automatically gain cult status.

FOR THE FILLING

- ⅓ cup plus 3 tablespoons / 120g pistachio cream
- ⅓ cup plus 2 tablespoons / 55g kataifi

FOR THE DOUGH

- Cooking spray, for coating the pans
- 1 cup (2 sticks) / 220g salted butter, softened
- 1 cup / 220g packed light brown sugar
- 1 cup / 200g granulated sugar
- 2 large eggs
- 2 teaspoons vanilla extract
- 3 cups / 375g all-purpose flour
- 1 teaspoon baking soda
- ½ teaspoon baking powder
- ½ teaspoon sea salt
- 12 oz / 340g dark chocolate chunks or semi-sweet chocolate chips

CONTINUED

WARM DUBAI CHOCOLATE CHUNK COOKIES, CONTINUED

Make the filling: Line a sheet pan with parchment paper.

In a small bowl, mix the pistachio cream with the kataifi until combined.

On the prepared pan, form 20 dollops (about 1½ teaspoons each) of the pistachio mixture. Make sure to use all of the filling. Flatten out the dollops a little with your palms to create discs. Place the pan in the freezer for at least 30 minutes or up to overnight. (This will make the filling firm and easier to handle during assembly.)

For the dough: Preheat the oven to 350°F / 175°C and spray three sheet pans with the cooking spray.

In a large bowl, combine the butter, brown sugar, and granulated sugar and, using an electric mixer, beat until light and fluffy, 3 to 4 minutes. Scrape the sides of the bowl with a spatula once during creaming.

Add the eggs one at a time, mixing well after each addition. Then add the vanilla and mix until fully incorporated. Scrape the bowl.

In a separate large bowl, whisk together the flour, baking soda, baking powder, and salt. Gradually add this dry mixture to the wet ingredients, mixing until just combined. Scrape and mix once more.

Fold in the chocolate chunks or chips until evenly combined. With a tablespoon, scoop balls of dough about 2.5 oz / 71g and place on the prepared pans. Then flatten each ball slightly with your palm. Remove the pistachio filling dollops from the freezer and place one in the center of each dough disc. Fold the dough around the filling to seal it completely. Ensure the filling is well enclosed and mound the dough high; it will spread upon baking. When all of the dough balls have filling, you can bake them immediately or freeze them until later. You will have about six to eight cookies on each sheet pan.

Bake for 14 to 16 minutes, until the edges are golden but the centers are still soft (it may take a few extra minutes if baking from frozen). The cookies will firm up as they cool.

Let the cookies cool on the pan for 5 minutes before transferring them to a wire rack. Cool for 15 more minutes before serving.

ACKNOWLEDGMENTS

Book baby number five! Every single page was a joy to work on with my editor, Cristina Garces, without whom *Après* would not have happened. We have so many more books in us.

Every writer knows the power of a great agent, and I'm lucky enough to count mine as a friend. Sally Ekus, your endless creative support—and that note you sent me when I really needed it: "For when you are ready"—makes me so grateful to you and sparks me every day. There's no one I'd rather have in my corner.

Thank you, Emma Campion, for your gorgeous design. To Erin Kunkel, for the beautiful photography and for allowing us access to your mountain retreat, Bonny Doon Cabin. To Vivian Lui, for making the food look as delicious as it tastes, and to Glenn Jenkins, for basically living in my head with those props! To Abby Oladipo for ensuring the book reads perfectly, and to Jane Chinn for production coordinating. To the unsung hero, editorial assistant Laine Whittier, for answering all my emails. To Emily Hotaling, marketing guru, for getting this book out into the world. And last but not least, to my awesome second editor, Kausaur Fahimuddin, for jumping in and bringing this project across the finish line. *Après* only exists because of all of you.

Thank you to my creative circle, the definition of women who really support other women: to the amazing producers Sarah Clagett, Rainy Farrell, and Jamie Nguyen, for letting my creations shine on screen. To Amy Goodman for always liking and sharing all my social stuff! To Jess Downey, the best brainstorming partner and *She WHAT?* co-host, and to Amy Lynn, for keeping me glo-ing.

To my home team, Mom and Dad: There aren't enough words in the world to express my love and gratitude. To Col (my favorite ice-skating partner); Dave and Christie; Daisy (my tireless and amazing caregiver) and Sean; and my fab in-laws, the Petroskys and Muñozes, thank you for all your love and support. Also, Dede, Nat, Lee Anne, Uncle Dan, Olivia, and Court, thank you for always showing up for me.

To Dr. Tamhankar, Dr. Pukenas, Laura Zarkoski, Dr. Ozoduguru, and the entire neurology team at the University of Pennsylvania, thank you for saving my life, giving me back my sight, and the ability to read and write again. It's hard for me to type that, but I can only do so because of you. You are angels on earth.

Michael, thank you for all the things—mostly for never doubting me (even for a single second), for holding me up from behind, and loving me in such a profound way I didn't know even existed.

My Scoops, Christo and El, you guys make me proud to be a mom. You know what I'm going to say, but I'm saying it anyway. Every day, start with gratitude. Be Big!

To all my friends, family, and supporters who buy my books, listen to the podcast, sign up for my classes, and are genuinely excited and happy to support my creative ventures (a few special shout-outs: Tara, Christy, Belinda, Sue, Vanessa, Stacy, Kiki, Keller, Krissy, Shan, Mis, Scrappy, Lee Lee, Claudia, Kimmy, and Jac), it means more than you know. Thank you all a million times over. There are more glitter, inspiration, and clinks coming your way.

XO, Maureen

INDEX

D

E

F

G

H

J

K

L

T

V

W

Z

TEN SPEED PRESS
An imprint of the Crown Publishing Group
A division of Penguin Random House LLC
1745 Broadway
New York, NY 10019
tenspeed.com
penguinrandomhouse.com

Typefaces: Monotype's Ambiguity and Bunny Dojo's Afire

Page 10: George Silk/The LIFE Picture
Page 14: Shutterstock Rave

Library of Congress Cataloging-in-Publication
Names: Petrosky, Maureen author
Title: Après ski : 75+ cozy winter recipes for the perfect post-ski gathering / byMaureen Petrosky.
Identifiers: LCCN 2025052520 (print) | LCCN 2025052521 (ebook) | ISBN 9798217273379 hardcover | ISBN 9798217273386 ebook
Subjects: LCSH: Cocktails | Snack foods | LCGFT: Cookbooks
Classification: LCC TX951 .P48579 2026 (print) | LCC TX951 (ebook) | DDC 641.5/3—dc23/eng/20260127
LC record available at https://lccn.loc.gov/2025052520
LC ebook record available at https://lccn.loc.gov/2025052521

ISBN 979-8-217-27337-9
Ebook ISBN 979-8-217-27338-6

Acquiring editor: Cristina Garces
Project editors: Cristina Garces and Kausaur Fahimuddin | Production editor: Abby Oladipo | Editorial assistant: Laine Whittier
Art Director and Designer: Emma Campion
Production designer: Mari Gill
Production: Jane Chinn
Food stylist: Vivian Lui
Prop stylist: Glenn Jenkins
Copy editor: Dolores York | Proofreaders: Alison Kerr Miller, Penelope Haynes, and Sarah Rutledge
Indexer: Elise Hess
Marketer: Emily Hotaling

Manufactured in China

10 9 8 7 6 5 4 3 2 1

First Edition

The authorized representative in the EU for product safety and compliance is Penguin Random House Ireland, Morrison Chambers, 32 Nassau Street, Dublin D02 YH68, Ireland, https://eu-contact.penguin.ie.